Equipping Y

TO DISCOVER the Genius IN YOUR CHILD

By Sharon Schnupp Kuepfer, B.A., B.Ed.
Illustrated by Ricky Martin

30 Days to Discover the Genius in Your Child:
Equipping Your Children for Life
by Sharon Schnupp Kuepfer,
B.A., B.Ed.

Artwork by Ricky Martin (rickydmartin.com)
All Scripture references are from the King James Version

Disclaimer: This book does not contain professional educational advice. Please talk to your local educator or school board about specifics.

Disclaimer: Various comments and conversations, as well as family archived journals/articles, may have been edited for brevity, clarity, and/or anonymity.

Library of Congress Number: 2021951873
International Standard Book Number: 978-1-60126-780-1

Masthof Press
219 Mill Road | Morgantown, PA 19543-9516
www.Masthof.com

To my children—

Kayla, Clarissa, Michael,
Nicole, and Natasha

—who allowed me to
"live the dream" by helping
them discover theirs.

Table of Contents

$340

LEMONADE

INTRODUCTION

Sharon's Background Story

You hold in your hands a book that has been years in the making. You may wonder why I wanted to write on this topic. Let me begin by explaining a bit about my educational background. I've loved the learning process for as long as I can remember. When my sister and I played school, I was the teacher. But it didn't stop there—I graduated with an elementary teaching degree from Lakehead University. I then gained experience teaching classroom-style in both private and public schools for several years.

I always dreamed of homeschooling. But once we had children, it seemed sensible to begin their formal education in an ideal private school just down the road from where we lived in southern Ontario. However, our two oldest attended there for only a short time. Soon my dream to homeschool was fulfilled when we moved to Kenora, Ontario, and lived in the bush. We then homeschooled our children for many of their early schooling years.

For the younger grades, our homeschooled children did minimal traditional "schoolish" bookwork. To gain an even different perspective, on a year of sabbatical, all the children had the experience of attending mainstream public schools. By high school, most of their schooling was with the public educational system in one way or another. Along with that, though, we also did some high school courses "our" way, along the lines of their interests.

My educational philosophy was to allow children to school themselves as much as possible. (It isn't as bad as it sounds!) I had learned that cramming too much knowledge into children's brains wasn't the best way. Rather, I decided that a better goal would be to allow children the freedom to learn in their own way, at their own pace, along the lines of their own interests. That was my "idea," and I tried to do this as much as possible. Furthermore, I have always modeled this concept of pursuing interests—going by my passions and callings. This style of living has made for a fascinating and fulfilling family life!

For reader's ease, I have labeled my educational philosophy **SIFT (Sharon's Interest-Focused Teaching).** *The acronym* **SIFT** *articulates why I advocate the sifting of the unnecessary clutter around the idea of educating our children. Instead, I love the concept of getting down to what counts for our children and their learning.* **Interest-Focused** *describes our emphasis on child-led, curiosity-based living and educating by following the interests of the child.* **Teaching** *refers to how, regardless of the educational setting, we as parents are continually called to be teachers of our children. The following Bible verse indicates this mandate:*

> *"And thou shalt love the Lord thy God with all thine heart, and with all thy soul, and with all thy might. And these words, which I command thee this day, shall be in thine heart. And thou shalt teach them diligently unto thy children, and shalt talk of them when thou sittest in thine house, and when thou walkest by the way, and when thou liest down, and when thou risest up" (Deut. 6:5-7).*

Our children survived—and thrived—in our **SIFT** program, and they have all gone on to post-secondary education in various directions beyond high school. For some skeptical folks, this fact might give a bit of proof that our **SIFT** program worked. My children, by and large, enjoyed our style of schooling. The icing on the cake is that the next generation is also interested in utilizing the **SIFT** schooling method. My daughter has already started teaching her young children, incorporating the ideas from this program into their lives.

THIS BOOK WITH THE 30-DAY PROGRAM

Many years ago, I was inspired to make an easy plan for moms to implement my **SIFT** methodology, which I was trying to do with my children. This desire resulted in a bare-bones draft of this 30-Day **SIFT** curriculum, which I had written on a trip when our five children were ages 6-13. The point of 30 days was to create a doable, bite-sized project for folks to learn the concepts. However, the ultimate goal is to weave the **SIFT** methodology into daily activities so that this way of living becomes a lifestyle.

Obviously, this **30 Days to Discover the Genius in Your Child** project has been on the back burner for years. Occasionally I would dream about getting this book ready for the public. Then in 2017 and 2018, I compiled various ideas and stories for a series of Facebook posts that supported my **SIFT** method. I did this by pulling information from our archives of scribbled notes and journal-type entries, which I patched together the best I could to make them readable. I believe the concepts brought out in our family's experiences can be helpful to any growing family. These stories are from approximately a three-year period (my children's ages will be indicated in each story).

The real-life stories were added to my 30-Day curriculum in March 2020 when the COVID-19 pandemic hit in full swing. I would see moms on Facebook talking about being "forced" into homeschooling. I thought of my program and decided that offering it now could be helpful to young moms and valuable to me to develop my curriculum further.

Hence, I ran this program twice as a Facebook private group in April 2020 and again in May 2020. It was a real asset to my bare-bones curriculum to add those Facebook-shared real-life early chronicles about our family, showing how my **SIFT** ideas worked.

It spurred me on later that year when my son Michael said, "You should write a book called, *How to Raise Your Kids in a Stimulating Environment*."

Here, then, in your hands is the result of the above long, drawn-out process!

WHO IS THE *SIFT* 30-DAY PROGRAM FOR?

This written curriculum in a conversational style is from one mom to another (though fathers and children and teachers, or anyone, are welcome to "listen in" and glean ideas ☺). More specifically, these concepts are:

1. For moms interested in helping their children discover their passions and gifts; the result will hopefully be equipping children with tools to find a life's vocation they love. The young generation may be able to unearth the unique way they can be of service to others, polishing their talents for God.

2. For moms interested in helping their children find ways of studying that fit their learning style.

3. For any family, no matter what method of educating is chosen. The **SIFT** program detailed in this book can be used by all parents, whether the selected method is traditional schooling, homeschooling, or a mixture. Parents are called to be teachers of their offspring, even when others help in the process.

A few years ago, a young schoolteacher said to me, "I've been reading your homeschooling philosophy posts on Facebook. I thought it would be good to incorporate your ideas into my classroom; however, it seems easier to simply do the bookwork."

I agree that it would be more challenging in a school setting to go by our style, but it's still worth a try! When I was a teacher in a regular classroom, I attempted outside-the-box activities. Why not have fun and incorporate some of these ideas? If you do, I'd love to hear your stories.

~ Sharon

WHAT THE *SIFT* 30-DAY PROGRAM IS NOT INTENDED FOR

It is *not* to help moms/children select specific textbooks, curriculums, school schedules, subjects/concepts to cover when and for how long, or any other "schoolish," more concrete details. Having said that, it is possible that readers may be able to glean ideas from my 30-Day **SIFT** program that could shed light on some of these specifics.

WHAT THE *SIFT* 30-DAY PROGRAM IS INTENDED FOR

To **inspire** moms to provide children with what they need to learn, allowing the youngsters to follow their interests. Then "let them go," simply observing and recording what your children are learning and doing. We are all different in how much "relaxed" schooling and/or parenting we are willing to allow, but my main takeaway is "as much as possible."

To **inspire** children to pursue their God-given interests and explore the environment around them, with lots of free time and lots of freedom to encounter "experiential learning" as much as possible.

In a dreamy, airy, nebulous sort of way, to **inspire** moms and children to be willing to "sit with" lots of mystery. To trust the process, to trust ourselves, and ultimately to trust God.

WHAT ABOUT GAPS IN THE *SIFT* METHOD?

Some people might wonder about concepts that could be missed by doing the **SIFT** style. I am not too worried about "gaps" in learning ☺. Our experience and belief is that what children "miss" (and every educational setting will have gaps!) can quickly be learned by taking advantage of your local public school's summer programs when the student is ready and needs it.

You just need to dive in!

> *I can see this taking off with moms and teachers. It's basically opening our eyes to see what the child is already doing and building on that.*
>
> *~ Debby Ropp, educator*

PREFACE

How the SIFT Program Works

This 30-day curriculum is for moms of children with ages ranging from pre-school (or you could go as low as age 2) to high school. I would encourage moms to use a buddy system, where you do this program with one or more interested, like-minded moms. There's nothing like support for fun and fellowship.

I will give a different assignment each day for each of the 30 days. Most of the assignments take ten minutes, with some exceptions. On days when more time is needed, just do what you can. Like all of life, the more you put into something, the more you get out of it.

For each assignment during the 30 days, you will be asked to write down your children's spontaneous activities. For some of the assignments, other research is also suggested. Each day you will start with a new blank page per child in your "Discover the Genius in Your Child" binder (see below in the "Materials Needed" section). Here you will write down what you observe in your children, in whatever length or format works for you. At the top of the clean sheet, write whatever day you are on, such as "Day 1" or "Day 2." This daily practice of being aware of your children's activities, interests, and giftings will help you understand each child better and be a documentation of their learning. You may do "free journaling" as well—whatever helps you to incorporate the **SIFT** method into your lifestyle. Take into consideration your personality and style when recording your children's activities so that you can stay in a "fun" mode, rather than you dreading recording the assignments. After implementing the **SIFT** program, you will have 30 days' worth of data for each child.

Our family's real-life stories hopefully help bring substance and understanding to the program. Various references or "quotes" mostly from me, but also from other folks, are sprinkled throughout as support for my **SIFT** ideas.

I suggest running this program for 30 consecutive days—the momentum will be fun and motivational. You know there is a limit and end! If you fall behind, rather than trying to catch up and getting discouraged, I encourage you to just jump in on the day you are ready for, rather than feeling "behind" all the time. Later, you can always come back and do activities after the 30 days are over. Again, interacting with your like-minded friends can be a helpful way to do this project.

SUGGESTED GUIDELINES FOR THE 30-DAY *SIFT* PROGRAM

At first glance, this style might seem very unstructured and loose, as if the child is in charge of their life. However, these are guidelines I suggest:

1. Each child should continue performing their regular chores.
2. Each child should get up on time and eat meals together with the family if possible.
3. Each child needs to continue to respect all family members, especially the parents.
4. What I'm *not* promoting is for a child to be "in charge." (That's not good—every child needs to know that they are not the kingpin in the family.)

5. Limited or no television, videos, or computer games.

    a. An exception would be if you sense that your child could be interested in a future career in the technology industry. But even then, the issue of becoming a "couch potato" could hinder you in discovering their wider giftings. Hence, during this month, I would encourage at least limiting exposure to technology.

    b. If your children have had a steady diet of technology filling their spare time, it may take them a little bit to grow back into using their imagination. You might find that your children don't know what to do with technology-free time, and it will take them some time to adjust.

A NOTE ON PARTICIPANTS' COMMENTS

I include participants' comments from my two online courses anonymously and with their permission, hoping that these thoughts from other moms can benefit those of you who are doing this 30-day program. Additionally, I'm incorporating many of my daughter Clarissa's comments, as she took the two online courses in 2020. My writing through the years has first been for my children's benefit. (They are the "audience" I always have in mind. Then if other people are blessed, so be it!) Now that my daughter is in this stage of life with her two children, I decided that this is an excellent time to push forward with writing the curriculum, which has finally, at long last, turned into a book. Many of her comments concern her daughter, Evelyn, at the age of 2 and are incorporated in this course. Their son, Emmett, is also mentioned, but since he was a baby, he was too young to be really included as being "in school." So, it's exciting and fulfilling to see that my free style of educating is staying alive through the generations.

MATERIALS NEEDED FOR THE ASSIGNMENTS FOR THE 30-DAY *SIFT* PROGRAM

Materials:

- Large three-ring binder labeled on the front "Discover the Genius in Your Child," with as many inside dividers needed to separate the number of children you are observing this month
- Package of three-hole lined paper
- Clear pocket folders (one per child) that fit into a three-ring binder where you can store some of each child's memorabilia collected during the month (to be used on Day 7 and then up to the end of the 30 days)
- Four various-colored highlighters (to be used on Day 9 and then up to the end of the 30 days)
- Timer

OR, with our modern era, one could simply make use of all these materials on your phones/computers.

A participant of my online course suggested that perhaps moms might want to focus on *one* child for the 30-day period. I think that is a personal preference, so I will leave that up to you. I would say it depends on the amount of time you have and want to put into this program. I would still favor doing all your children simultaneously and just gauging how much time you have for the assignments.

SUGGESTED READING LIST

Here is my highly recommended, though optional, reading book list for further help in understanding my **SIFT** method. You can't read all these books in one month, but I am listing them here for you to obtain and read ahead of time. Optionally, you can choose to do the course first and read these books in the future.

They are excellent reading material for any family educational library to help understand our program about your children's learning. These books seem to focus on homeschooling; however, many ideas can be gleaned no matter your educational style.

Enjoy!

- *How Children Learn* by John Holt (or any of his books)
- *Homeschooling for Excellence* by David and Micki Colfax
- *The Successful Homeschool Family Handbook* by Raymond and Dorothy Moore
- My (Sharon's) two books on our family homeschooling experiences (can be ordered from my website www.skuepfer.com)

    1. *Homeschooling Moments and Child-Friendly Recipes: A Collection of the Unique Adventures of a Mennonite Family*

    2. *There's No Place Like Home: Tales and Treats from a Mennonite Family*

Years ago, my sister told her husband how reading Homeschooling Moments and Child-Friendly Recipes *inspired her in her homeschooling. Her husband commented, "Reading this book is like going to a homeschool convention and gleaning all kinds of things, but it is all wrapped up in one book." And I say, thank you, brother-in-law, for the commendation!*

~ Sharon

BIOGRAPHY OF
The Kuepfer Family

Kuepfer family summer 2020: Left to right: Rachelle and Michael Kuepfer, Steve and Sharon Kuepfer, Eric and Clarissa (Kuepfer) Byler with Evelyn (2) and Emmett (8 months), Kayla Kuepfer, Nicole Kuepfer, Natasha Kuepfer (Photo credit: Mark Petersheim)

Steve and Sharon Kuepfer: We married in 1989 and in 10 years had our five children. In 1999 we moved to Kenora, Ontario, to do ministry work in the Kenora Jail. We are still here and loving it!

Kayla graduated with her 4-year Bachelor of Education and has since worked in several schools in various roles. She especially loves working with special-needs children. She lives in Kenora, Ontario.

Clarissa graduated as a Registered Practical Nurse (RPN) and then married **Eric** Byler. They have two children, **Evelyn** and **Emmett**. They live in southern Ontario, where Eric is working on his master's degree in counseling.

Michael is currently working on his master's degree in counseling. He is married to **Rachelle**, and they run a lawn care business in the summers. They live in Kenora, Ontario.

Nicole is currently working on her Bachelor of Arts, with an interest in counseling and/or social work. She lives in southern Ontario.

Natasha is a student at the University of Waterloo in a general degree, with an interest in social work. She lives in southern Ontario.

2001 photo from approximately the time period when many of the stories in this book took place. Kuepfer Parents: Steve and Sharon. Children in order of age: Kayla (10), Clarissa (8), Michael (6), Nicole (3, on right), and Natasha (3, on left) (Photo credit: unknown)

Kuepfer Children

Foreword

My Father's Version of "Finding Your Children's Genius"

For years, my dad has been a passionate teacher of family values and godly parenting. Recently, I mentioned to him how he used to teach about the verse, "Train up a child in the way he should go: and when he is old, he will not depart from it" (Prov. 22:6). I remembered it had something to do with a natural bent each child has.

My father responded, "Everyone has different personalities and interests, so parents need to spend time individually with each child to be able to hear their concerns and desires. Have a plan in your head for each one."

I went on to ask Dad, "Wouldn't you used to say when you would teach on family life, 'Don't treat your children all the same?'"

I remembered Dad saying long ago that a couple had once told him about how their one child wasn't doing very well.

They then told Dad, "We treated them all the same."

My father said he replied to them, "That's why there's a problem. You need to treat children differently according to their innate abilities, what was born into them, and listen to what they are interested in."

That's how Dad tried to work with his five daughters. In this recent conversation with Dad, he told me, "During a certain time of your young lives, one afternoon a month, I would meet with a different one of you girls for an hour. I would ask about your interests, such as sewing or painting. This was in order to have quality time with each daughter, to help you girls verbalize and process your ambitions and desires. I bought each of you children a three-ring binder 'life notebook' for you to record your ideas and goals for life. As young girls, your dreams were fluid and would change from time to time, depending on your age and interests. These changes would show up in the record books."

Dad concluded, "I don't have a cut and dried answer to all this, but these are some ideas that might help you."

What Opa (Grandpa) says about not treating your children all the same applies to more than just education. Reading this almost made me cry.

~ Rachelle, my daughter-in-law

This is so good—it's so true.

~ Nicole

DAY 1

Helping Your Children Find Their Genius

Further Details on the SIFT Method

Back in the early 2000s, after reading my email newsletter for homeschoolers, a subscriber responded, "I received both your homeschooling books for my birthday. I will have to admit, your children sound more industrious than mine."

I replied, "Each child has gifts, and it's important for parents to see what they are. What your children do probably won't be what my children do."

We are all different, and it might take time for you and your youngsters to discover their interests and giftings. When I was an adolescent, I remember feeling inferior to my friend because of her style of decorating her bedroom. It took years to discover my gifts, but now I feel comfortable with my home decorating style. The same thing happened in my writing career—it took years until I found my "voice." Give yourself and your children grace in the process of uncovering their genius.

How do parents help their children discover their innate gifts? I believe God created every child (hence, adults) to be creative, to find their "voice," as it were, in life. How does one do that? Here are some ideas that we have tried, and I encourage you to implement them throughout this 30-day program. This article fleshes out more ideas that I touched on at the beginning of this book, describing how to help your children follow their interests using the **SIFT** concepts.

- Set aside 30 days when your children can have lots of free time—summertime could be ideal for this.
- Work should be minimal and designated to a particular block of time. A lot of schoolwork or chores around the house can hinder inquisitiveness and curiosity. For example, children can develop habits of procrastination that rob precious moments. This wasted time could be used to do something creative. I'll never forget my sister's son years ago sitting on the bottom step at their house after he had been assigned the job of cleaning his room. This dear nephew of mine must have sat there for half an hour, dreading his five-minute job. I asked my sister, "How long are you going to go on like this?" My idea would be to offer an incentive or give a time limit, anything to let the poor boy get on with his interesting life.
- Plan for a time when your children can have plenty of time alone, without always being with friends. Socializing with friends is great, but it can also be so involving that the child has no time to explore their world. Friends can create all sorts of scenarios and peer pressure that can dampen the spirit.
- Let your children be uninterrupted. When they are following their passions, allow them freedom as much as possible. The great inventors needed lots of free time to explore their fields of interest and so do our children.
- Watch which activities absorb the most of your child's time. There may be interests that eventually could be used in their

career. While standing on the sidelines, also find out which activities have a common theme. My father's aptitude was mechanics, but then he ended up being a missionary. In his mission endeavors, however, one of his primary means of transportation involved aviation. His mechanical abilities came in handy while being a missionary bush pilot.

- Encourage. Many years ago, my father took me out to his workshop and showed me various tools that my then 8-year-old son could begin to use. "Your girls are businesspeople, but I think Michael needs something to help build his self-esteem and masculine ego," Dad informed me. When he was a youngster, my grandparents helped him find patterns for woodworking, and Dad then built various projects that he still owns today and wants to pass on to us girls when he's gone. Because of Dad's encouragement, Steve bought some tools. With these, Michael made wooden guns, hearts, and birds that we gave away as gifts.
- Provide materials and opportunities. As a youngster, Clarissa loved little children. One day it suited to invite a family with lots of children to come to play for the afternoon. I felt busy as it was, but I knew Clarissa would love it. Before we had finalized the babysitting plans, she had drawn up the following major chart:

Clarissa's Babysitting Schedule

1:40–2:10 Play
2:10–2:40 Naps (on another sheet she listed the ones who would nap)
2:40–3:20 Play outside
3:20–3:40 Coloring and songs and stories
3:40–4:20 Play and snack
4:20–4:35 Games (whatever you want)
4:35–4:45 Clean
4:45–5:00 Fun stuff outside
Done

- Don't be surprised at anything. One way to handle this is not to have goals or assumptions set in stone regarding your children's natural tendencies. For example, one of my daughters seemed interested in becoming a teacher, while my other daughter enjoyed babysitting. But back then, I wanted to keep my heart open in case something else showed up.
- Resist the urge to label interests as educational or not. One mother told me, "Your children have such 'schoolish' interests. My children's interests aren't educational." I think, though, that perhaps if she'd search, she'd see that there would be something useful in her children's "useless," seemingly non-educational ventures.
- Let their learning be in their area of interest. Years ago, my children went through a game-playing phase. They entertained themselves with these games morning, afternoon, and evening. The organization of cards and ordering of numbers was a great learning experience. What made it even better was the interest that naturally bubbled out of them—I wasn't telling them they had to do it.

As I said earlier, these points are listed to give readers guidance, particularly during the 30-day period. However, I did try to follow these tips as much as possible throughout our children's entire childhood.

Years back, when I was deep into discovering our own children's interests, I often found myself focusing on the topic—even while going about my everyday life. One day, while taking a bath, I thought, *Hey, I love this stuff so much that I could become a consultant to help others discover their child's genius.* I felt so passionate about this area of education, and I still do. That's why I'm writing this book.

Clarissa's Comments | When you talked about me wanting to be a babysitter, now in 2020, I'm having children. I thought that it was pretty interesting how it turned out. I also love the concepts in the above article. And of course, I loved being raised in this environment and want that for my children, too. When I observe Evelyn, I think about that. I like what you say, "Let their learning be in their area of interest."

Participant's Comments | I think that with homeschooling, some of these points are more easily facilitated. How do you balance chores (creating work ethic, responsibility, and discipline) with free time? I try to sprinkle it (school, chores, and free play) throughout the day. Then they don't have formal chore lists on the weekends. We also do a quiet time each day.

ASSIGNMENT FOR DAY 1

Now is the time to start using the binder you labeled "Discover the Genius in Your Child" filled with blank lined paper. Use one new page of three-hole lined paper per child. First, record "Day 1" at the top of the page. Underneath that, write down the child's name and the date. List the numbers 1–5 in the left-hand margin as shown below. Make this as simple or detailed as it fits your style. It can be handwritten or computerized. You can write three or more pages worth of notes or only one line. The point of the daily assignments is to learn to be more aware of what your children are doing.

Here is a sample of how yours could look:

DAY 1

Name of child______________________________
Date (day/month/year)________________________

Entry #	Time of day (e.g. 3:10 p.m.)	Description of Activity
1.		
2.		
3.		
4.		
5.		

Record each child's activities at five separate times in the day. Perform this task wherever you are at the moment—on a trip or at home. It can be done any day of the week or any season of the year. Don't discriminate whether an activity is educational or not. Just record and have fun discovering more about each child.

Below is an example from our family on a trip to southern Ontario, May 13, 2004. I created a chart combining all my children's activities to make it easier to view "at a glance." (Your chart will look different because each of your youngsters will be listed on a separate paper, like the sample above.)

"Whatsoever thy hand findeth to do, do it with thy might" (Ecc. 9:10a).

DAY 1: EXAMPLE

Time:	Kayla (13)	Clarissa (10)	Michael (9)	Nicole (6)	Natasha (6)
1. 11:43 am	-resting	-listening to tape about Louis Pasteur and playing doll at same time	-playing game with Natasha	-entertaining herself and looking out the window	-playing made-up game with Michael (she made the game up)
2. 12:16	-resting	-same as above	-resting	-"doing nothing" (according to her) -looking around	-playing game as mentioned above (by herself? I'm wondering as I'm completing the book!)
3. 1:55	-listening to story tape	-listening to story tape	-listening to story tape	-listening to story tape	-listening to story tape
4. 2:30	-practicing lines for play she made up (on her own initiative)	-practicing lines for play Kayla made up	-practicing lines for play Kayla made up	-practicing lines for play Kayla made up	-practicing lines for play Kayla made up
5. 3:00	-working on play	-asking, "What if someone would give us soup with minnows swimming in it?"	-eating fish candy	-eating candy	-eating candy

Clarissa's Comments | In the chart below, I detailed Evelyn's activities for Day 1:

ENTRY:	TIME:	ACTIVITY:
1.	1:35 p.m.	Evelyn is sitting on her bed cuddling Teddy Bear Otis (with her dolls lying beside her).
2.	2:10 p.m.	Evelyn is pushing her miniature wagon around and around on the dehumidifier and pushing it off it (like a ramp).
3.	3:15 p.m.	Evelyn has a little chair tipped over, and she is sitting on a stool by it. Then she walks to the bedroom and back singing "E-I-E-I-O" and keeps repeating this.
4.	3:50 p.m.	Evelyn is building a Lego house.
5.	4:30 p.m.	Evelyn is playing at her toy kitchen and has Dolly Tessa in the crib beside her and is holding Dolly Hope.

Another thing I noticed was Evelyn laying her blanket on the couch and lining up all her babies and teddies—then she sat there with them. Even between the times of recording Evelyn, I noticed that I was observing her more and seeing the different things she entertained herself with.

Participants' Comments

PARTICIPANT 1: It was interesting to notice my children's activities at certain times of the day and to see how they fit their ages. They're playing cars and creating a surprise birthday party for one of them. As much as I want their school and cleaning chores done, I think I need to let them play. I'm noticing how much they've learned in math by what they're playing, too.

PARTICIPANT 2: My boys do one main thing, and that is building roads and towns with blocks. They set up little people, so the times when I check in on them, they are always doing the same thing. And I know what they will be doing before I even check on them!

PARTICIPANT 3: My children got into fort building, complete with lighting (flashlights) and air conditioning (fans). Now I know that I cannot ask them to stop for workbook school (happy sigh). We will do schoolwork after lunch today because blanket forts are important, too.

Homeschooling has been a passion of mine, and I LOVED it during those years. As I mentioned earlier, our two oldest children first attended a private school for a short time. Then all five have gone to both mainstream public schools and made use of alternate public school programs as well. In all this, I am trying to say that there's no right or wrong way for children to learn, and the educational ideas promoted here can be applied while children are in any school program. Homeschooling, though, allows children greater freedom, especially if using the freer "unschooling" style.

~ Sharon

DAY 2

Observe Your Children and Keep Your Eyes Open!

Playing Motel

From back in my children's olden days, during our homeschooling years, I have a purple file folder recording times that all five played "Motel."

Recently, I dug in this folder and unearthed what I had penned back then: "The house got cleaned, as the entire house is the motel. No one complained much about cleaning up tonight."

I had a relaxing evening because I wrote that I came up to my bedroom and put my feet up on the easy chair. (Nice!)

I noted that Michael (6) signed into the motel, and Kayla (10), the front desk lady, said, "Here's your card. You have room #3."

I heard Natasha (4) tell Michael, "I forgot to give my money to Kayla."

Clarissa (8) announced on their toy loudspeaker, "Dinner's ready in an hour! Dinner's ready in an hour!" She then asked, "Mommy, can I make soup?" This was going to represent a full-scale motel, including soup in the restaurant.

"Sure," I said.

During one of these motel-playing episodes, a sign-in sheet recorded in the section of "how long" each stay was to be, the following:

Clarissa: 2 months (Wow!)
Natasha: 5 months (Really?)

Now, in their adult world, three of my daughters have worked in the motel industry, and I would say, quite enjoyed it for a time.

Their play did become their (adult) paid employment!

As an update, Natasha said recently, "'Motel' was one of my favorite things to do. When Kayla got older and wasn't as into it, I was kind of sad."

ASSIGNMENT FOR DAY 2

Pick a time in the morning, such as 10:00 a.m., to see what activity each child is doing. Record this entry on a blank page in your "Discover the Genius in Your Child" binder, writing "Day 2" at the top. Detail what your youngster is doing at that specific time. If you have more than one child, and if it fits the situation, watch for, and then journal who is the leader, follower, loudest, peacemaker, and so on. Tailor your writing about each child to fit your personality and style. One sentence is fine, but so is a whole page and any length in between.

Clarissa's Comments | Concerning children exploring their interests and hobbies on their own, I see it so much in Evelyn. She uses a lot of imagination and creativity in her play. I often wonder how ideas come to her like the wind. It's all part of the learning.

"I will instruct thee and teach thee in the way which thou shalt go" (Ps. 32:8a).

Participant's Comments | I like to think back to my older children's early play. One of them, in particular, showed so much of his core self in his play—he lined up his toy cars and proceeded to "fix" them. I thought he might be mimicking his dad—he is a mechanic. My son looked so dedicated, and this reminded me of his dad.

TO MOMS DURING COVID-19: please don't be too hard on yourself if you're suddenly being asked to educate your kiddos in some semblance at home. They won't suffer from a temporary lapse in more structured learning. They learn automatically, even in play.

~ Maria Miller Rockhill, my childhood friend and author of Peace by Piece.

DAY 3

Educating Through the Years

Would I Homeschool the Unstructured Style All Over Again?

Recently a friend who visited me asked, "So, looking back, would you homeschool the way you did it all over again?"

"Yes!" I said.

There's no question in my mind. I can't think of much that I would change, except to have trusted my God-given instinct more—to "let my children go" even more on their own timetable without me worrying about their future education.

At the time, it was hard to go against the grain. How did I know if my children would learn the things they needed to learn?

Well, I just tried to follow my heart, even in moments of doubt. As I was the main "teacher" in our home, my hubby trusted me to do what I thought would work.

Later, another friend visited, and we chatted about our homeschooling days.

"The way you did schooling was more doing it according to your children's interests," she said. "It was your own curriculum, wasn't it? Would have been a lot of work!"

I replied, "It was so much of a passion for me that it didn't feel like work."

Recently my sister asked me to help formulate a curriculum for her daughter in high school, whom they were homeschooling part-time that year. So, I dug out all my stuff—our provincial curriculum guidelines as well as timesheets of how my daughters recorded their time on their various subjects. The result was that my sister got a free consultation from me! I loved it, and it seemed to help her.

And for me and mine, the **SIFT** style was a delightful way of learning, which is why I wrote my first two homeschooling books about this process. A generation later, it thrills me that my daughter is incorporating this method with their growing family. (She did emphasize, "In our own way, of course!")

> **Participant's Comments** | We finally decided we are ready to homeschool. I feel more loyal to traditional schooling because I loved classroom learning. But it is looking more and more likely that we'll be jumping into homeschooling next year and would follow our children's interests, too. The one thing I lack is courage.

ASSIGNMENT FOR DAY 3

Sit down with a cup of tea and decide what you want your children to have learned by the time they're 17 or 18 (end of high school age). Journal these thoughts on a clean page labeled "Day 3" in your "Discover the Genius in Your Child" binder. If you're a busy mom and all you have is a short time, just ten minutes (if you don't count making your tea ☺) is okay. Even jotting a few sentences is enough. You may record more general goals or specific, measurable ones. Some general ideas to journal could include your children knowing the basics of cooking, playing the piano, and being responsible adults. Optionally, you could be more specific, as I describe in my example below:

> "Shew me thy ways, O Lord" (Ps. 25:4a).

I wanted all my children to have a high school diploma or an equivalent so they'd be prepared for college or university in case they wanted to further their education. Preferably, I wanted them to have thirty credits, which is what is necessary for students to receive a high school diploma in our province.

Finally, record one activity that your child performs spontaneously at some point today.

Participants' Comments

PARTICIPANT 1: I always pictured homeschooling as being boring ☺. But even as a young girl, I knew the Kuepfer homeschoolers learned lots and, I assumed, had fun while doing it ☺. Also, every time we came to your house, I was amazed at the many books, charts, and graphs in your school area ☺.

PARTICIPANT 2: This assignment was fun. I'm sure I could've been more specific per child—I did just a quick generalization for all the children. It impressed upon me the importance of making each day count, and it was just good to write down goals.

First and foremost, our responsibility as parents is to help our children become the people God wants them to be—to be the best servants for Him.

~ Sharon

DAY 4

Don't Rush Children

Laid-Back Living

One thing that came through a couple of times in looking through my old file labeled *How to Homeschool and Make It Look Easy* is how my mother said she potty trained us girls. She would try it, and if it didn't click, she'd let it go and then would attempt it a month or two later. Simple dimple.

I applied this philosophy as well to other areas of child training. If something didn't work, I would attempt to do things another way or come back at a later date. And I tried not to be pressured by what other people thought. This laid-back style meant that our children were generally not the earliest to catch on, whether with potty training or learning to read.

For example, in this same old file, I recorded how Nicole's interest in writing happened. One morning, when I came back home after being gone for a few hours, preschooler Nicole proudly showed me how she was practicing writing her name. "See how I hold my pen!" Later, Nicole had practiced writing her name on sixteen papers—I counted. The sheets were large, mostly blank, but with some writing on each.

Her identical twin, Natasha, had been writing her name for a while already, with great interest. Nicole, however, simply had not been motivated at that time but rather had shown more interest in drawing or doing other things. She was her own person, thank-you, even though an identical twin.

But now, writing her name fascinated her!

Apparently, I was gone again later in the day. (Wow, I went out a lot back then! I think I've since become a homebody!) Once again, I found sixteen more (though mostly very small) papers lying around, this time with more writing per page of various letters of the alphabet.

So, this was Nicole's day to shine!

And isn't that a good thing? That even though the two girls are so much the same, they are still unique individuals with their own timetables of learning and pursuing their interests?

Because all of a sudden, Nicole's interest in writing came.

And she's loved writing ever since! Recently, she's even started her own blog.

I'm sure glad, looking back, that I allowed the difference to happen.

And I tell you—it's waaaayy easier to feel confident about these things, now, after the fact, as we see how our young adult children have survived and thrived—hopefully!—with our parenting and schooling style. I want to assure you, readers, that you too will not "ruin" your children if you let them develop on their own schedule. All children are gifted—that's because we are all made in the image of God. And we have a creative Creator!

Michael's Unrushed Schooling

Recently, Michael asked me, "Remember when I was in school for that one year (grade five), and they had me in special ed for a bit? Was that because of the way you and Dad didn't believe in pushing us?"

My answer was, "Yes, for sure!"

He went on to say, "The other day, our neighbor asked me, 'Is school hard?' I didn't get a chance to answer, but I was going to say, 'No, it's not hard. I'm breezing through my master's degree in counseling.'"

So, he came unto his own. In his own time. At his own pace. Yay!

~ Sharon

Participant's Comments | The reminder to wait until they're ready is good for me. It's easy to rate where my child should be based on others his age. I just potty trained our 3-year-old, who is our third child. It's the first time I've waited so long to do this, and it was SO easy. We could still have some regression, but it feels like he's got it. Where did the idea come from that around age 2 is ideal? Anyway, I need to remember this perspective when homeschooling, too.

ASSIGNMENT FOR DAY 4

Record one afternoon entry per child on a clean page labeled "Day 4" in your "Discover the Genius in Your Child" binder. Choose a time slot beforehand, such as 2:00 p.m. Write down one activity per child. Your entry might read "napping" for John or "emailing" for Sally. Or it could be a very detailed record. The entry length can depend on how complicated your child's task is or how much you enjoy writing. Tailor these journaling exercises to what fits your mood and style. Resist the urge to make this project too complicated. Otherwise, you might be tempted to give up.

"O Lord; teach me thy paths" (Ps. 25:4b).

Clarissa's Comments | I looked out the window and watched Evelyn proudly watering the flower beds, which she had just watched her daddy do earlier. Then she ran inside and said, "Mommy, come, I watered garden." She proceeded to take me all around the house to show me her flower beds and point at the wet around the flowers.

*The **SIFT** program creates an awareness in us as moms. The saying goes, "What you focus on increases." If we keep our eyes open to our children's giftings and encourage them along lines of their interests, it will give them a better chance to thrive in their learning and in life.*

~ Sharon

DAY 5

Allowing Creativity

Creative Juices

Early in 2002, Kayla (10) got her creative juices going for a club that included Clarissa (8), Michael (6), Natasha (4), and Nicole (4). I unearthed the following from an old purple file where Kayla had penned the following brainchild, which was based on the book series called *Secret Seven*, a favorite of our children.

> Good morning. We are going to start a club. It is called Secret Five. We are going to do lots of fun stuff. We are going to have meetings quite often. We are going to wear a badge. And we are also going to have a password that means if we ever want to get into our clubhouse, you have to say the password. We are going to call our password "fantastic." We are going to change our password every week. To learn more about this club, I am going to read you a book called the *Secret Seven*. That is where I got the idea of this club. While I'm reading you this book, you may have a snack.

On the other side of the page, Kayla's writing continues. I guess part of the club was earning money!

When we earn money at winter:

1. Work for mom
2. Work for dad
3. Bake cookies

Summer:

1. Sell cookies
2. Sell lemonade
3. Have a garage sale

What we want to buy with our money we are going to earn:

1. Craft stuff
2. Dress stuff

What we want to do:

1. Hide treasures
2. Do plays and puppet shows and sing
3. Do crafts
4. Sell stuff and earn money
5. Have a meeting quite often

On a new page, Kayla planned their second meeting.

> Good morning, Secret Five. This is our second meeting in this cubbyhole clubhouse. Since it has snowed, we will have our meeting in here instead of the teepee. Our password is still "fantastic," but next time we have a meeting, it will be "teepee." Does everybody think that is a good password? Natasha and Nicole, you may color this picture of Winnie the Pooh while I read to Clarissa and Michael from the *Secret Seven*. But first of all, we will talk a bit.
>
> Ok, I have to tell you something about our badge. You may write our password on your hand. We will call it our badge. Now we may talk about whatever we want to, and Clarissa can get our candies now.

End of Kayla's description of their club. Eventually, I assume they moved on to planning another club or adventure.

So, that was that.

I still love it when any of my (now all adult) children (or in-laws!) tell me one of their creative ideas. For example, Clarissa recently said that when Eric, her husband, saw a marble roller for fifty cents at a garage sale, he knew he wanted one. Having loved this activity as a young boy, he now bought it so that he could play with his children.

Participant's Comment | Sharing the results like this is so impactful because we can see the benefits of your style of educating.

ASSIGNMENT FOR DAY 5

Play Mozart or some other soothing background music.

In your binder "Discover the Genius in Your Child," start a clean sheet of paper per child, writing "Day 5" at the top, as well as their names and date as you did before. Set a timer for one hour. Don't work longer unless you are absolutely enthralled. You want this to be fun, not drudgery. In this one-hour period, record whatever activities your children are doing. You may do household work or whatever in between writing, but try to keep recording their activities off and on during this hour.

"I am the Lord thy God, which brought thee out of the land of Egypt: open thy mouth wide, and I will fill it" (Ps. 81:10). *If that isn't amazing, what is?!*

What to watch for:

- posture
- tone of voice (talkative, quiet, voice volume)
- boredom versus excitement
- anything else that strikes your fancy

If they come to you during this hour saying they are bored, tell them to try to find something to do. This lack of enthusiasm for life can come from too much traditional school, chores, computer time, videos, or time with peers. It may take a while for them to get into the flow of following their interests.

Clarissa's Comments | It was interesting watching Evelyn for the hour. It was during her "quiet time" in her room. She went from building her Lego house to having her tea and toast to putting socks on herself and then, later on, to singing the ABC song and rocking her teddy and repeating lots of that.

Participant's Comments | Even though my children played with Legos the whole hour, it was fascinating to listen closely to what they were doing and saying. I think I could've gone longer than an hour!

Remember, you can try this new and different ***SIFT*** *approach for a month. If you don't like it, you can go back to the "old" way after these 30 days!*

~ Sharon

DAY 6

"School" Through Life

Can Baking Count as School?

Many years ago, I announced (according to my record in the old manila folder labeled *There's No Place Like Home*), "No school today."

I pronounced this as the beginning of the Christmas holidays.

I then said, "Baking today." My announcement seemed to please Clarissa (9), as by 8:15, she was softening butter in the microwave for rolled Christmas cookies.

The baking continued, and somewhere along the way, Natasha (4) became her sidekick.

They made:

1. Christmas cookies (They baked one sheet of cookies, then put the rest of the dough in the fridge. This is one of my theories—if they get tired of a project, they can stop, coming back to it later. In this case, the baking of the cookies could be finished another time.)
2. A double batch of finger jello for our Christmas dinner.

Mid-morning, in the middle of this flurry of food-making, Clarissa and Natasha decided that they would additionally make a fancy restaurant lunch for Nicole (4) and Michael (7).

Clarissa came to me in the office and said, "Come, I want to show you something."

I followed her. She pointed to a step-stool at the entrance to the kitchen. "This is where we write the people's names, and then they sit down. Then I come to Michael, and I say, 'We have water, ice tea, lemonade, and strawberry kiwi. What would you like?'" Then she said she'd write in her little book what they wanted.

Ok!

With some help from their dad—and a can of stew—shortly after 11 a.m., the big "restaurant-opening" moment arrived. Part of their plan was for Natasha, with her serving apron on, to come slithering out from under a blanket that covered a kitchen chair when Clarissa called, "Natasha!"

I penned at the time, "Not sure what effect this was to produce, but it added to the mystery of this venture that all morning Natasha and Clarissa had worked hard on (secretly)."

"Can I order two stuff?" Michael asked when presented with the four drink options (typical boy!).

The meal progressed and must have ended successfully, as I didn't record more details.

So, another morning came and went in our fun homeschooling days.

Back then, I wondered, did they do "school?"

On the baking day, I recorded the following educational documentation (more for Clarissa, as Natasha was so young):

- ...reading recipes: reading comprehension
- ...math: measurement (cups, teaspoons, etc.)
- ...health and safety: "Make sure you use the back burner—that's one of my rules," I insisted. (It's safer than using a front one where the pot could more easily get bumped off.)
- ...active participation: Clarissa's baking partner was Natasha, so they coordinated operations.
- ...delegation: Clarissa told Natasha what to do.
- ...time management: They worked from around 8:15-11:15 a.m.

And the great finale was when I wrote that they cleaned up (in their childish way) their messes.

Wow!

Bringing us to the present, these adult daughters of mine still love to bake and cook.

Participant's Comments | I well remember the days when I was at your place, and your children baked or cooked. I also remember thinking that was how I was going to be when I had children. Unfortunately, I don't know if I will ever be as relaxed and chill about the chaos in the kitchen as you were. I try! It just doesn't come naturally, and it's so much easier just to do it myself.

MY CONVERSATION WITH A PARTICIPANT

PARTICIPANT: I love your personal examples and stories! It's so fun to see how everyday life is teaching and can fit into what we've "book-learned." We're just getting to the stage where our son can read recipes and help cook simple foods, but our children have helped in the kitchen since they were little. Sometimes I feel guilty for cooking or baking without them because I want them to learn and enjoy it. But it takes much less energy to do it alone.

SHARON: Each mom needs to decide how to do things and how much she can handle. My mom allowed messes, and she wasn't super structured, so I had that model. My only recommendation is to involve them when you want to and have the energy. Having them learn at a young age was good for my children. It also came in handy when they got older and mostly took over my household and baking jobs.

PARTICIPANT: Ok, good. I feel like I have so many questions. I'm already excited to see how your *30 Days to Discover the Genius in Your Child* book turns out! I'm thinking it would be a great baby gift for new moms.

You mentioned letting your children stop and come back to finish baking. This is something my husband and I both struggle with. We tend to want them to finish something they've started—a game, a project, etc. What's the balance of teaching them within their age range and attention span while still encouraging them not to quit but rather to persevere with a task?

SHARON: This is a tricky and interesting question. For me, with my personality, I get bored pretty quickly with a task. I will stop halfway through a job if I'm bored or want to do something else and will come back to it later. For example, I might start something in my writing career, as I did with this *30 Days to Discover the Genius in Your Child* book and put it down to finish later. I began writing this back in 2004 and am only finishing it now that my daughter is a parent. I'm not a big one to say you have to finish something just because you started the task, necessarily. But that's me, and you are the expert on yourself and your children. My advice would be to bend a little bit in this "relaxed" way for a month and see what you think by the end of the program.

ASSIGNMENT FOR DAY 6

Play Mozart or some other soothing background music. On a fresh page in your "Discover the Genius in Your Child" binder, briefly record two evening activities that your child performs spontaneously. Consider how their activities could possibly fit into a "schoolish" category, such as I penned in the above baking story.

Clarissa's Comments | In the evening, we were outside. There were so many activities I could have recorded besides the two I did. I felt I was more aware and observing the many things Evelyn entertained herself with. Children are fascinating, and I often wonder how Evelyn comes up with the next thing she does. She loves it outside and is normally happy the whole time she is out there.

"Train up a child in the way he should go: and when he is old, he will not depart from it" (Prov. 22:6).

Participants' Comments

PARTICIPANT 1: I was intrigued with the idea of just letting them quit a job and finish later.

PARTICIPANT 2: I'm actually really, really enjoying this. It's providing a lot of food for thought. And, yeah, I'm very intrigued by it, especially watching what they gravitate toward.

I think I have a lot to learn about my children. I really like clues on how to pick up on what they like—and realizing that I don't have to be so structured in my theories of finishing the job and putting everything away.

MY CONVERSATION WITH A PARTICIPANT

PARTICIPANT: I realize that I kind of fear or dread their boredom. I would be interested in more direction on how to help them solve it instead of me just trying to give them work or feeling frustrated when they get bored.

SHARON: What might happen if you'd allow some space for them to figure it out? Try trusting them.

Give your children their childhoods back. Let them decide what they do and when. Allow them to get bored until they come up with "the next thing" and watch expectantly to see what that activity is—then run to your record book and scribble away. The **SIFT** *lifestyle is a blast!*

~ Sharon

FUN FINGER JELLO

Whisk:

2½ cups water
1½ cup fresh or frozen strawberries, quartered
3 tablespoons unflavored gelatin

Bring to a gentle boil, stirring frequently.
Pour into blender and blend.*
Strain juice (use cheesecloth if you want a very thin liquid), discarding pulp.

Whisk into above mixture:

1 teaspoon fruit extract (such as raspberry, but any fruit extract can be used)
a couple dashes of stevia (or another sweetener of choice)

Taste test and add more flavor and/or sweetener as desired.
Pour mixture into glass 8 by 8 pan and refrigerate until set. Don't be surprised if foam rises to top. Cut into squares.

** Parents should help small children with the blending process because the liquid is so hot.*

DAY 7

Children and Earning Money

Business Ventures

I wrote about Michael (6) and his business interests in an old green homeschooling file folder. He said to me, "I like it when you are in my room, talking to me." (Does having a listening ear help children's creativity by allowing them to process out loud?)

Michael was thinking about "earning money" during many of his waking moments. He'd been pestering me, asking what he could do for me to make some money. I gave him odd jobs—cleaning, packaging, and babysitting—(babysitting who? I wonder as I type this from the old file. I figure it meant his 3-year-old twin sisters, and it makes me wonder how they enjoyed his 6-year-old babysitting skills). For Steve he shoveled snow.

Michael said, "I'm proud 'cause I'm selling cookbooks." (Not too long before, I had finally found a place for him to sell some cookbooks put out by our organization.)

Later that day, he commented, "Mom, remember when Kayla and Clarissa had a little store in our house?"

How well I remembered! It was a good idea and experience, but it didn't really fly.

"I should have a store," he said.

I talked him out of that idea but rather encouraged him to get things together for a garage sale, so off he set to sort toy trucks and cars for the next half hour.

A while later, he came into my room and saw a gallon jar half-full of pennies. Our neighbors had given it to our children so they could roll the pennies into penny-paper rolls to be exchanged for cash at the bank. The jar had been sitting there for a while. Michael's older sisters had rolled some but then had lost interest in the project.

Now, Michael came along with his business mind, and I laughed. He was hard at work, while his mother was exhausted. He had enough energy to spare, as he rolled \$1, \$2, \$3, then \$4 worth of pennies. Well, this boy was off to be a businessman!

At one point, he showed me how he was learning to speed up his penny-rolling production—he put eight rolls in the lid of his gallon jar.

"Then I go 'drun, drun,'" demonstrating how he shoveled the money into the penny-roll papers.

Clarissa (8) came upon the money-making schemer and exclaimed, "He's probably going to finish all the pennies! That's no fair!" She was frustrated with her energetic, business-minded brother.

By quitting time, he had rolled $18 worth of pennies.

In exchange for the $18 worth of pennies, I gave him $18 cash to put in his bank account.

He said, "Mommy, how much do I have now in my bank?"

He checked in his bank book (adding on the $18 from the pennies), then he yelled to his dad as he ran into the kitchen, "I almost have $91!"

After Michael started yet another business venture a few weeks later, his money-making inspiration seemed to be catchy.

Nicole said, "Mommy, how can I earn money?"

Oh, dear.

So, she and her sister began rolling pennies.

Hmm. And no wonder I would get tired!

Tada. Now, so many years later, it's Clarissa's turn to inspire her children to become businesspeople.

Participant's Comments | This article got me brainstorming. Currently, my 7-year-old son has a little card-making business. He makes six, and then he takes pictures of them. Next, I post them on Facebook, and he's sold thirty so far. He's filling an order right now. I vacillate between wanting to remind him to work on them versus seeing when he gravitates toward it. Who knows how long it will last, and I don't want to force him to do it. He says he likes it.

ASSIGNMENT FOR DAY 7

In your children's clear pocket folders in the "Discover the Genius in Your Child" binder, begin a collection of their memorabilia. Today, put in at least one item per child, such as notes that they wrote, pictures colored, a bulletin of a program attended, a small stone, or a bird's feather they found. Continue to collect such items in their clear pocket folders until the end of this 30-day program. Always be alert for themes coming through.

"Ask, and it shall be given unto you; seek, and ye shall find" (Matt. 7:7a).

Sometime today, record two activities for each child in your "Discover the Genius in Your Child" binder. The theme of "earning money" might not necessarily come up today, but keep your ears peeled for the possibility if it does. Perhaps your child isn't interested in making money today, but they might be tomorrow. Children are often fascinated with business opportunities.

Clarissa's Comments | I love these assignments. I watched Evelyn play outside for over an hour, and it was fascinating to see what she came up with next. She loves exploring.

After supper, she wanted to write and then explained that she stenciled an "E" for Emmett and one for Evelyn. After she went to bed, I looked closely at it and was so fascinated to see what a 2½-year-old "writes," as she referred to it.

Mom provided us girls with a stimulating environment, presenting us with various ideas or projects. We were left to our own devices much of the time, yet somehow she managed to supervise us fully.

~ Sharon

DAY 8

Freewheelin' Schooling

A Smashing Success

Below is a story that I scribbled down eighteen years ago about my sister Carolyn's relaxed homeschooling style. At the time she thought it wasn't successful, but in the end, it turned out that it was! The other day, I read this article to her over the phone, and she cried. I told her that this story embodies my homeschooling philosophy.

My sister's success story is "proven" by all their older children having gone on to further education after high school. (I'm saying this in case she or any of you need the "proof of their pudding!")

> My 13-year-old niece came to my place for a few days. Her mom, Carolyn, and I have always been close. As children, we played school, and I taught her to write in cursive. She attributes her sloppy writing to my teaching. I am older by two and a half years, so she admired my knowledge.
>
> Thirty years later, her homeschooled daughter came to visit, and I was impressed. My sister would describe her homeschooling as rather unstructured and loose, with the children having plenty of time to pursue their interests. This relaxed schooling has had my sister unrelaxed at times. Their hectic missionary lifestyle leaves her

slightly anxious—what kind of scholars would their school produce? Or do you even call it school?

I'm here to tell you that she needn't have worried. Being around her daughter these few days, it hit me that this child-turning-woman could converse with most anyone on most any topic. She can babysit, save money, and stand up with a true and brave character.

How has she acquired this?

As a family, they've traveled extensively in the States and Canada. They eat a variety of foods. "We just finished up our deer and elk," she told me. She's dabbled in calligraphy, doll making, and stamp collecting. There's not a lot she hasn't done. She plans to take a hunter's safety course once her 11-year-old brother is old enough. She's like an adult in the kitchen. If she doesn't know the answer, she'll find out. One morning she called her dad to see how he makes his thrifty omelets. She can swim, play volleyball, ride a horse, and I'm sure she could drive a car if she'd be allowed behind the wheel.

The day before we journeyed the eighteen hours to return her home, she asked, "Sharon, do you have any books for me to read on the trip?"

Confidently, I marched her into the living room. I pointed out a book. No, she'd read that one. And that one, too. "What about *What Katy Did?*" I asked. No, she'd read that one and *What Katy Didn't Do* and *What Katy Should've Done* (or whatever those titles are). Like an eagle circling its prey, she prowled the house for a find. I couldn't believe a 13-year-old having read such a great variety of books. Finally, I found a 600-page old classic that satisfied her post-grade-twelve reading level. Good. At least I accomplished my job. How did her mother manage to keep her supplied?

My version is, let her skip high school, and then she can enter university with no problem and with no high school burnout. Why do I say this? Because with her wide experience, broad knowledge base, and encompassing worldview, she is educating herself.

You needn't have worried, Sister. Your homeschool has turned out to be a smashing success!

If you would like more ideas on how we homeschooled, you can get the gist of it here in the above little write-up—freewheelin', active, lots of outdoor play, and exploring their interests and environment. I wanted our home to be a haven where children could simply be children. One of the biggest things was that I had fun along with them, and homeschooling was never a chore for me (well, except that parenting is "hard work," if you look at it that way!).

ASSIGNMENT FOR DAY 8

Reread your random journal entries per child so far in your "Discover the Genius in Your Child" binder. Can you spot a particular time of the day when your children are more productive? Jot down any pattern like this that you see emerging in each child.

For example, I'm a morning person. Evenings I tend to shut down, but sometimes I do get a second wind. Late one night, when I was waiting up for Steve to come home, I worked on setting up my website.

Briefly record one activity that your child performs spontaneously today.

"For I know the thoughts that I think toward you, saith the Lord, thoughts of peace, and not of evil" (Jer. 29:11a).

Clarissa's Comments | Although Evelyn is still so young, I notice that she definitely is the happiest and plays best in the morning. Her quiet time recharges her, but after supper, I can tell she is done in. It's interesting that even though she doesn't often nap anymore, she is so happy during and after her quiet time. If she misses that, the rest of the day is harder.

If you are a homeschooling mother, try for a day, or week, or month, to homeschool by doing nothing. Rather, use the "watch, wait, and see approach" to see what might be developing inside your children. If you have youngsters in a school setting, I suggest figuring out a way to use this "watch, wait, and see" approach as much as possible and in whatever way you can.

~ Sharon

DAY 9

Organization to Help the Flow

Charts and Life

In a manila folder from the era of our homeschooling days, I have charts of various shapes, sizes, and details.

I found:

...a bedtime chart
...a couple school charts/schedules
...a "morning first thing before you come down" chart
...numerous chore charts

In more recent years, I still love charts and lists:

...chore list for when the family is all together
...chart of stuff that needs to be done to keep this house in some sort of order
...prayer list

These tools help me live life well.

But I'm realizing more and more that life can't always be managed with charts. It seems like often I have NO CLUE what to do in certain situations. But lately, instead of analyzing and philosophizing and worrying, I am leaning more toward simply trusting God to show me what to do.

It's easier than all that hullabaloo!

Yet, for the practical side of life, I still love charts. So, I guess, as in everything else in life, there's a balance.

Participant's Comments | I identify with loving charts and lists. I've been trying to decipher which of my children find lists motivating and which find it bothersome. I appreciate the reminder that these are tools and that living by the Holy Spirit is the ultimate over lists.

ASSIGNMENT FOR DAY 9

In your "Discover the Genius in Your Child" binder, use your highlighters to highlight any areas from previous days that seem to fall under any of the following four categories. Suggested colors per subject area are below:

- YELLOW HIGHLIGHTER: Language Arts (such as Reading, Writing, Spelling, Creative Writing)
- BLUE HIGHLIGHTER: Arithmetic

- GREEN HIGHLIGHTER: Environmental Studies (Science, Social Studies, Technology) *Note: for the older grades, the terminology could be "History" and "Geography"*
- ORANGE HIGHLIGHTER: The Arts (Music, Drama, Art)

Note: In the same manner and as applicable, continue highlighting during the remaining days' recording assignments for the rest of this program.

Additionally, record one activity your child did on their own initiative for the longest period of time.

"And thine ears shall hear a word behind thee, saying, This is the way, walk ye in it" (Is. 30:21a).

Clarissa's Comments | One theme I noticed a lot was music—Evelyn is often singing. She sings songs she likes, such as "Old MacDonald" and "Twinkle Twinkle," as well as songs she makes up. Sometimes she even mixes different songs together. I remember John Holt talking about this in his book *How Children Learn*—that often young children make up songs or mix a few together. Evelyn has loved playing Legos the past few months too, and I often record her building stuff. What I find so cool about this is that her building Legos could be considered science, math, and art. Three different areas! I went back with my highlighter and put in all three colors with her Lego building.

Participants' Comments

PARTICIPANT 1: Finally, a way to use my highlighters! As I was going through my notes today, I realized that I don't feel like I really handled an opportune moment correctly. My son had told me he noticed that every time a crow caws, it moves its whole body. But now, because I noticed it, maybe I will catch it quicker next time, and we can talk about it rather than me saying, "Just get to your schoolwork."

I don't think I will highlight the Legos because that will be pretty much everything. But it could be most of the colors! I did highlight a specific Lego area where I felt they were doing math.

PARTICIPANT 2: This was a fun assignment. Apparently, my son is mainly into music and drama. He is obsessed with David and Goliath and will act it out in his own way. Also, I often hear him quietly singing while playing, but there are many times when it's not so quiet as he strums his little guitar with enthusiasm.

If you were hoping for a pat answer, such as, "Here's how to do it," this isn't the course for that. My **SIFT** *approach involves mystery and allows for differences in opinions and people and parents and parenting styles. It's not "one size fits all." Rather, it's "try this and try that." By the end of the month, if you feel a little freer (and hopefully your children will too!), if you allow more messes, if you are observing your children rather than pigeonholing them into a specific mold or a certain curriculum or whatever, then my goal as an educational consultant will have been accomplished!*

~ Sharon

DAY 10

Messes Are Necessary to Create Masterpieces

Making a Mess

Clarissa said recently, "Mom, when I read through your books you wrote about us, I wonder where we children got all our creativity from."

Well, part of my **SIFT** philosophy is that mommies shouldn't worry children overly much about cleaning up after messy play, as that can stifle creativity. I obviously worked on the tidying-up issue, but I didn't want to make that so all-important that it discouraged my children.

I wrote the following story years ago, which I recently unearthed in an old yellow folder, which shows one way I handled "children cleaning up messes" (or not!).

Kayla (11) and Clarissa (9) worked hard on preparing a "Bible School" in our Kenora kitchen for Michael (7), Nicole (5), and Natasha (5).

They had a "bees" theme, and their color was yellow—"because bees are yellow."

They had collected a stack of books...

- ...a yellow joke book (because it's yellow)
- ..."B" world book
- ..."poems and prayers for the very young" book (has a bee poem in it)
- ...children's encyclopedia (with a picture of a bee)
- ...child craft book (story about bees)

A metal tray containing various yellow objects sat on a stool, such as a yellow pencil crayon, yellow chalk, and a yellow toy.

Kayla explained to me, "We're playing a game. These are all yellow. You show it and then take it away, and they have to see how many of these things they remember."

The word "yellow" was on a flashcard.

On the table were pictures of bees to color, with crayons and pencil crayons.

Clarissa rehearsed a poem for me that she and Kayla had made up.

I wrote in my journal, "This is an organized and well-thought-out project. It also gives me a much-needed break."

At 6:17 p.m., they rang the "Bible school" bell.

Then I heard "Jesus Loves Me" wafting from the clean kitchen into the office where I sat. (The laundry room, however, was a sight to behold—the floor cluttered with little toys, some coloring books, a few bins, scrap papers, towels, and a bag of Kayla and Clarissa's knitting.)

I heard Kayla and Clarissa reciting a verse in unison to their class, not concerning themselves with any laundry-room messes.

Halfway through the session, Clarissa came into the office and moaned, "Mom, Michael is being real bad and

getting the twins to be bad." I gave her a suggestion of what she could try with him.

On the kitchen marker board, Kayla had a fill-in-the-letters puzzle, with the "answer key" being "I love Bible school."

However, Michael seemed to have a different idea, as at the end of the class, he said, "That was a dumb club."

Clarissa was upset about this, so I told her, "Next time, don't have Michael in it." I mean, why force a boy to do a "fun" project?

The following day, I came down to a mess in the kitchen—a cluttered table with a rumpled tablecloth, scattered pencil crayons, red candy wrappers on the floor, chairs haphazardly placed, pretzels on the floor, and coloring pictures of bees on the table.

I thought, *I might as well just clean it up.* The older ones had entertained the younger ones (and themselves)

> while Steve had been gone for a few hours in the evening. And it only took me about five minutes to get most of it back in place.

I assume that my children still make messes to get their masterpieces!

ASSIGNMENT FOR DAY 10

Sometime during their waking hours, in your "Discover the Genius in Your Child" binder, for ten minutes record your children's spontaneous activities, meaning ones *they* have chosen. Watch specifically for random things like facial expressions or tone of voice in their conversations with others. Make sure to write the time of day you are journaling.

"Call unto me, and I will answer thee, and shew thee great and mighty things, which thou knowest not" (Jer. 33:3).

Participant's Comments | My 3-year-old brought some rocks into the house. Normally I would say, "Keep the rocks outside." But I realized, *I can accept these rocks and be okay with it.*

> *Mom didn't give a rip about messes. She gave us free rein in her kitchen, and, for better or for worse, she didn't expect us to do tons of chores. She somehow expected us not to get bored. Hence, we had time and freedom to use our imaginations.*
>
> *~ Sharon*

DAY 11

Local Educational Requirements

Broaden Your View

A homeschooling friend Facebooked me the following question:

"I read your post about you helping your sister make a plan for her high school student. I wondered if you would consider helping me do the same thing for my last child. My child just started high school and has never enjoyed school. I would be so glad if I could find something that would be enjoyable for my high schooler while still learning and doing the necessary schoolwork."

The following is the gist of how I answered her:

1. Find out what is required by law in your area. I like to think that if I could satisfy the requirements with "my style of relaxed schooling," then I would be so happy.

2. Discover what your child is interested in. Ask them what they would like to learn and/or do in school and for their fu-

ture. Also, you might want to share with your offspring your own ideas of what they could do with their time and studies.

3. If possible, keep the option open for the child to enroll in a formal school setting. For our children and us, we have always liked to prepare for this, and we were glad we did. All our children did end up graduating with a provincially recognized high school diploma, having the requirements needed to enter university/college.

Actually, this last step might not be all that important. For example, when the children were still in high school, I told my youngest daughters that if for some reason they didn't have all their official grade twelve credits, they could always do a summer course at the local public school to upgrade.

So, for my friend, and for you, my readers, at least the above is a start to exploring your options!

ASSIGNMENT FOR DAY 11

Find out what requirements by law you need to report as homeschoolers in your province or state. Even if your children are in a regular school program, research more about your child's requirements. It will help you understand your offspring's future schooling better. Go online or call the local public library for information. As the children get older, knowing their interests could help you guide them in choosing electives to take in high school. Record any findings in your "Discover the Genius in Your Child" binder.

"Knock, and it shall be opened unto you" (Matt. 7:7b).

Journal two of your children's self-initiated activities today.

Clarissa's Comments | I enjoyed researching. This helps me get ahead of myself since Evelyn is so young. Plus, I told Eric I can always go to you for lots of advice. I was at it for twenty to thirty minutes. I didn't want to stop because I was having so much fun.

Participants' Comments

PARTICIPANT 1: I'm going to say something here to keep me accountable—my goal for next week is to research my state's regulations!

PARTICIPANT 2: I took this course last month, and the above assignment motivated me to contact the evaluator I wanted to use. Doing the course this second time around, I can now say that the evaluator is a great resource.

I will never forget going to a homeschool convention in Winnipeg while we were still homeschooling. A home-school mom got up to talk about how she helped her son get from homeschooling through high school into his acceptance at university. I knew she was more of a free-style educator when she said, "Remember, when you are recording the activities your child does into the various subject categories for credits, EVERYTHING IS SCHOOL!" (I remember thinking, **Well, everything except sleeping!** *Yet, there is much benefit in that too, but I'm just not sure how to relate that to school!)*

By the way, homeschooling conventions are AWESOME!

~ Sharon

DAY 12

Varied Opportunities

Helping Fulfill Your Child's Dreams

Clarissa (8) had seen a young teen playing mandolin at a children's program. Afterward, for weeks on end, she kept asking for one.

Finally, one day I got on the stick and called all over Winnipeg, trying to locate a mandolin for my daughter. No one had any, at least not at the present.

Another day, then, I phoned in to our local "Swap and Shop" via radio, nervously asking, "I would like a mandolin."

Immediately, I got a call from the second-hand store in town. I went to look at the mandolin, and I even received a free lesson from the dude. He taught me three beginner chords, which turned out to be very similar to those on a guitar.

Later, Clarissa and her dad went to town to pick up the mandolin. Two-hundred dollars poorer, they walked out of the store. I ordered Clarissa a book with a recording, and soon she began chording on the instrument during our family devotions.

You know, I love it when children (or adults!) follow their dreams and pursue God-given desires, but it does take work for the parents!

ASSIGNMENT FOR DAY 12

Sometime during your children's waking hours, in your "Discover the Genius in Your Child" binder, for ten minutes record their spontaneous activities—ones *they* have chosen. Take notice if one child is more detailed and organized, while another one might think and play with more freedom.

Clarissa's Comments | I brought out paper dolls for Evelyn to play with today—ones from my childhood that I played with somewhere under the age of 10. There were dolls I had cut out from magazines and made clothes for out of colored cardstock paper. Evelyn was so excited to have paper dolls. I watched her learn how to put clothes on them and fold the paper to make the clothing stay on.

Also, in her world of play, I've been observing how Evelyn watches me and does what I do. The other day I got out the jolly jumper for Emmett, and there was a little pillow attached that looked like my nursing pillow. Evelyn was so excited and promptly got set up on her chair with her "nursing pillow that matches mommy's" and "nursed" her teddy, Otis, all wrapped up in blankets. Later, as I walked around with Emmett, swaddled up, and put him to sleep, she swaddled Otis and walked around patting him like I was doing with Emmett. It reminded me again of John Holt's book *How Children Learn.*

"Lo, children are an heritage of the Lord" (Ps. 127:3a).

He said something along the lines that imagination or fantasy is children's way of entering into the adult world as they are watching us and doing what we do.

Participant's Comments | My children have spent the last half hour playing in a mud puddle. My daughter, who loves to sing, made up a song while playing. The 11- and 9-year-old boys are more interested in playing with the hose that makes the mud. And my toddler used his hands a lot in the mud, quietly doing his own thing.

Being exposed to a variety of opportunities broadens a child's view. I learned this from my dad and mom, as they signed me up for piano, guitar, canoe, flying an airplane, and pottery lessons.

My parents also offered to pay for a counselor if we girls, as teens, so desired. I probably milked that cow more than any of my sisters.

As we homeschooled, I never liked the idea of children being cooped up within four walls with intense workbook learning—and where the teacher happens to be the mother. That scenario didn't make sense, at least in our situation. (By the way, I worry about the modern video schooling where children sit so many hours in front of a screen.)

Getting out with the local homeschool group and also with other families was a fun part of our program. Socialization IS important!

Our aim as parents was for a broad worldview.

~ Sharon

DAY 13

Life Learning Through Money-Making

Busy in Business

This is another story about Michael (6) and his interest in earning money years ago.

A few weeks after his penny-rolling business plan, he was still asking, "Mom, how can I make money?"

So, I was telling my sister about this, and she said that a store close to her was having a great sale on crafty little canoes. Perhaps Michael could paint them, fill them with wild rice, and sell them.

Oh!

So, the process began.

It seemed to take great effort on my part—as I turned my kitchen countertop, at least part of it, into a workshop for businessman Michael. He hired 8-year-old Clarissa (IF THEY WOULD SELL!) to help him with the painting, and she thought this was awesome. The canoes were painted purple (much to their father's amazement—shocking color, I guess, for a canoe) and some blue and red, with several paddles painted yellow, and I don't know what else.

Steve asked at lunch, "Do you think they will sell?"

"Of course," I answered, very sure of myself. We would have to see.

The problem with this venture was I would hear, "Mom, get the twins out of here! They are bumping the chair!" Keeping the little ones out of the way was indeed a problem, as usually they were being entertained by these recently-turned-businesspeople.

There was paint on the side of the cupboard, the floor, the countertop, and purple and yellow paint splotched on Michael's navy shirt.

On the same morning, Kayla (10) wanted to sew. I informed her that as we had just gotten home from a trip, I was POOPED, and not in the mood to help her sew.

"What about an apron?" she asked.

Well, that sounded reasonable, so I explained where the material was and not to use my good dress material. In the end, without too much help from me and making up a pattern as she went, Kayla sewed a cute, crafty-looking apron.

I said, "You know, Kayla, it wouldn't take too much to make aprons for sale."

Help! Did I really say that? Not another tiring business plan!

A few days later, I recorded in my old homeschooling file that the canoe business kept progressing, as the paint was slathered on and getting better with each one. One canoe was finished off with wild rice in a little bag in the bottom, packaged up with raffia on the top, with two paddles attached to the raffia.

Part of the marketing plan was to attach a recipe for *Wonderful Wild Rice Soup* to the canoe. Before selling these canoes, Michael needed to "test" the recipe.

Making this soup, in his mind, was not as thrilling as the painting part.

He then sold his first finished canoe to my bookstore friend. Three others were placed in his favorite place for sales—in a Kenora restaurant ("We'll see if they sell," I had penned back then), and his uncle was buying three more.

Things were coming along.

Several weeks later, Michael had sold two canoes at the Kenora restaurant.

Accomplishment!

Oh, the joys of mothering.

But I also wrote, "Sometimes I get tired."

Yet, years later, I saw Michael as a young entrepreneur, running his own (summer) lawn care business (and paying his way through university) and owning his own lawn tractor, push mower, weed trimmer, and trailer. And loving it!

Well...

That's all the thanks this mother needed!

ASSIGNMENT FOR DAY 13

Discuss and plan one way each child can earn money. Record any plans in your "Discover the Genius in Your Child" binder.

The following are some ideas from the good ole days:

- *I paid Kayla (13) for vacuuming instead of me paying someone else. (The best idea, however, is somehow for the children to bring money into the family, as discussed below.)*

- *Michael (9) sold woodcrafts at a restaurant's checkout counter. My sister-in-law bought a popsicle stick airplane he had made.*

- *One summer Kayla (12) and Clarissa (10) babysat for mothers who attended a neighbor's Bible study.*

- *Clarissa (10) wrote a storybook. She never published it, but years later, as a young adult, she wrote several articles for publication, building on her prior writing experience.*

- *My mom liked to get my children to clean her house, and she paid them a bit.*

- *Kayla (13) and Clarissa (11) pulled weeds one summer for a neighbor.*

- *Clarissa (11) sold her homemade candles at the end of our lane. Kayla, Clarissa, and Michael have had various bake sales. From one of the garage and bake sales, Kayla (11) received a commission to make bread and buns for a neighbor lady on a regular basis.*

- *Michael (11) was the CEO of the "greenhouse business" with Nicole (8) and Natasha (8) as his employees. They would sell pepper and tomato plants at the end of the driveway (having grown them from seeds). Michael had taken over the business from Kayla and Clarissa, who had raised and sold a variety of plants, but the process began to indicate that tomato and pepper plants were the most profitable. Then, when Michael was 14, he moved on to new and faster ways of earning money. After that, Nicole (11) and Natasha (11) took over the business, which they honed to perfection (until they moved on to new things!)*

Additionally, record one activity your child did on their own initiative for the longest period of time in your "Discover the Genius in Your Child" binder.

Clarissa's Comments | It's fun thinking about this. Evelyn could sell cards or do little projects around the house to earn money.

Participant's Comments | My middle son found a Lego set that he really wanted, which was $10, but he didn't have enough money. I usually just try to push those things off and tell them they don't need more Legos, but this time I told him he could do some jobs and try to earn some more cash. He then proceeded to do lots of chores for me until I was running out of ideas. He earned enough for the Lego set! I just happened to be going to town that day and found the set he wanted. It felt like a good thing for him that day. It reminded me so much of the stories in Sharon's book, *There's No Place Like Home,* that I had to share.

"Is anything too hard for the Lord? At the time appointed I will return unto thee, according to the time of life, and Sarah shall have a son" (Gen. 18:14). *God spoke these words to 99-year-old Abraham.*

Recently, Michael said, "Following my interests as a child and having a free childhood helped me to start my own lawn care business at age 20."

I remember his aunt as well as his dad's friend being shocked that Michael, at such a young age, had started his own business.

~ Sharon

WONDERFUL WILD RICE SOUP

Brown in frying pan:

1 lb. ground beef

Put into large pot.

Add:

2 cups sliced carrots
½ cup chopped celery
2 cups tomatoes
2 cups potatoes, cut up
⅛ teaspoon salt
2 beef bouillon cubes
½ cup chopped onion
¼ cup wild rice
6 cups water

Simmer for about 45 minutes, or until vegetables are tender. Serve hot, with fresh bannock.

DAY 14

Recording Life as School

Smiley Face Club

Going by the idea that "everything is school," here's a "school" story called "Smiley Face Club" that I recorded in the good ole homeschooling days many moons ago.

This club was 9-year-old Clarissa's brainchild, and her junior club mates were Nicole (5) and Natasha (5).

At the time, I wrote, "This really helps me because it certainly entertains the twins."

On this particular day, they had a Smiley Face Club presentation for some of the rest of us. Nicole held up a sign indicating $3.40 to show how much money they had earned in their offering. The show was, at least in part, a fundraiser. (For what? I have no clue!) As Nicole passed the offering bucket around, they also sang one song for the audience, a song for the offering, and a smiley face goodbye song. We clapped.

After the show, Clarissa asked, as she held up a sheet of stickers with smiley faces, "How many of these can I use to decorate our offering bucket?"

She's already getting ready for the next club meeting as she wrote down the words for a new song.

She asked, "When we go shopping, what can I buy for the Smiley Face Club?"

Clarissa estimated she'd had 10 or 12 Smiley Face Clubs so far. The participants usually got candy for participating.

A week or so later, this club was still going, and Clarissa asked me, "Mom, do you know how the twins learned the Ten Commandments last time? By these little smiley face people."

I asked, "How?"

"Well, first of all, I had this preacher come out, and he asked the commandments," she said. "Each of the twins knew one."

She was meticulously drawing little heads on a stand and ended up with twenty-three little people.

"They're mostly heads, aren't they?" I asked Clarissa.

"No, they're smiley faces."

Oh!

So, could "school" in this story be recorded as writing, reading, oral and visual communication, along with music?

If so, there you go!

Easy peasy!

And fun.

Though one of the best things is, I didn't have bored children! And currently, none of them are usually too bored!

ASSIGNMENT FOR DAY 14

Sometime during their waking hours, in your "Discover the Genius in Your Child" binder, record for ten minutes your children's spontaneous activities—ones *they* have chosen. Use your highlighters to highlight any areas that seem to fall under any of the four subject categories listed in "Assignment for Day 9."

"...become as little children..." (Matt. 18:3).

Clarissa's Comments | I love recording Evelyn's activities. One theme I see coming through is her artistic interest—she loves singing, drawing, cutting, and coloring. Also, her artsy leanings show as well when she builds Lego structures or serves many pretty-looking dishes with her "toy food." All those activities could also be included in other "school subjects" besides art.

Participant's Comments | How's climbing in and out of our bi-level house's basement windows categorized? My boys felt quite smug about their "brainy" idea.

"Fun" Viewed and Recorded as "School"

In my How to Homeschool and Make It Look Easy folder, I recorded that in July 2002, I found the following paper on a clipboard, written in Kayla's (11) handwriting:

Title: Town Outside
Doctor and dentist: Clarissa
Bank and library: Kayla
Church, store, and gas station: Michael
Garage money people: Nicole and Natasha

As Kayla and the others got older, they became more interested in increasing their "schoolish" type studies. However, her piece of paper I found still fits well with one of my philosophies—"that learning can be fun."

~ Sharon

DAY 15

Learning About Money Matters

Can Games Teach Money Skills?

Is playing Monopoly "school?" I questioned back in 2002, during our fun homeschooling days.

I must have decided it was because I had written on Michael's (7) school chart to play Monopoly with Nicole (4) and Natasha (4).

So, one morning a game was started. And it happened that Michael landed on Kentucky.

"Rent!" Nicole called.

I helped Michael read that he owed her "eighteen dollars."

He looked at his money. He started counting his 1s. Only five. Then he put the 1s back and stared at his money. Now what?

He took a ten and kept shuffling his money back and forth until all on his own, he came up with one ten, one five, and three ones.

I laughed so hard (quietly) that I wiped the tears. If I would have told him which bills to pick, it wouldn't have been nearly as effective. To see the lights blink on as I watched was sooo exciting.

Soon, Natasha slid onto Kentucky, and Michael was able to help her get the $18 just like that.

Not long before this game happened, I had scanned one of my niece's "real" school letters home to her parents. It read, "Play games at home like Monopoly."

And I shout, "Yes!"

Because children love games and children love working with money, why not combine the two and count this as school?

Currently, they as adults still play games—though I'm not sure they consider it school!

Participant's Comments | My boys play games a lot. The second oldest really likes them, so I've figured they qualify as education. This has me thinking about how games could continue to be in his education.

ASSIGNMENT FOR DAY 15

Open a savings account at the bank for each of your children. If it doesn't fit into your schedule today, mark it in your day planner for another day. Second best, set up a sort of family account at home that acts as a bank. Money matters seem to fascinate children of all personalities. Putting the responsibility in their hands—the younger, the better—is the key. Record how this went in your "Discover the Genius in Your Child" binder.

"Wealth gotten by vanity shall be diminished: but he that gathereth by labor shall increase" (Prov. 13:11).

For us, I began to teach some of them at a young age how to record finances. Once when Michael was a youngster, he went to the bank, and the teller got mixed up, writing the wrong amount that Michael had deposited. We knew it was an error because in little boy scrawled handwriting, Michael had written $100 in his bank book before he had gone into the bank. But this all was a good experience, teaching him basic life skills.

Record two of your children's spontaneous activities today.

Clarissa's Comment | Eric started a savings account for Evelyn a while ago ☺!

Participant's Comments | We started a savings account for our oldest at age 6. We haven't done it for the next one yet. I hadn't thought of getting them to keep records yet, though. I'm glad you're touching on this topic!

For homeschooling, like the rest of parenting, we have one chance (for a period of time) to give it our best shot. My homeschooling shot is over. I am relieved, on one hand, yet kinda nostalgic on the other. But if I can help anyone with my experience, that would make me almost as happy as doing it myself!

~ Sharon

DAY 16

Thinking Outside the Box

Can Older Children Teach the Younger?

Back when we were homeschooling, I was inspired by hearing about older students teaching younger ones.

Ok.

So, one day, I offered Clarissa (9) and Michael (7) five dollars to share to buy anything they wanted once Michael learned to recognize and say the upper- and lower-case letters of the alphabet. The stipulation was he needed to do this very quickly and at random.

Up to that point, he had been very unmotivated to learn these. I had read that a child doesn't necessarily need to know each letter's name before they learn sounds and begin reading. However, I felt like he was plenty old enough for learning his alphabet.

The twosome began.

As I observed Teacher Clarissa, I found that she did just as well as I would have. It was an excellent review of the alphabet for her and training her to think through how to teach these. When you teach something, you really get to know the subject.

I heard Clarissa say, "Okay, write down the letters you already know."

Wow, I thought, *what a great teaching concept!*

Then at one point, though highly motivated with the idea of spending five dollars at the local store, Michael was wearing out.

Clarissa came to me, discouraged, and said, "Michael isn't even trying."

I said, "As a teacher, you need to think of something different." I gave her an idea to try.

In the living room, she scattered cards with letters of the alphabet on the floor, and he could step on letters he knew.

One and a half hours later, I realized that they both had fun. I had a blast as well watching one of my favorite hobbies—the delegation of duties for the best of all parties.

Of course, I was there as a background supervisor, but I was able to get a lot accomplished on my sewing project while they rattled off the ABCs around me.

Maybe Clarissa's teaching paid off, as present-day Michael is still involved with the letters of the alphabet—he's in school to become a counselor and lovin' it! Sometimes, though, it takes a long time to see a payoff!

Clarissa's Comments | I love this concept of older teaching younger. All on her own doing, Evelyn was singing *Old MacDonald Had a Farm* to Emmett. She had a book open with farm animals. As she sang about the different ones, she would take his hand and point at that animal on the page that she had been singing about.

Participants' Comments

PARTICIPANT 1: I love this aspect of homeschooling. It can keep all ages entertained and older ones feeling like leaders.

PARTICIPANT 2: Love the alphabet idea with a sibling. Gotta try this!

ASSIGNMENT FOR DAY 16

Sometime during their waking hours, in your "Discover the Genius in Your Child" binder, for ten minutes record your children's spontaneous activities—ones *they* have chosen. Think about how your children are getting along with each other. Further, notice if one child is helping or "teaching" a younger sibling. To clarify, I think this older teaching younger can be good, but I'm not promoting on a general basis that the older should boss the younger.

"...suffer little children, and forbid them not, to come unto me: for of such is the kingdom of heaven" (Matt. 19:14).

Clarissa's Comments | Today I recorded that Evelyn asked for my camera and proceeded to take pictures of me holding Emmett. Then she went around and took many other pictures. She put her toy truck on the floor and took a picture with a little person in it. Eric and I were both so impressed with her photography. When we looked through her pictures, she excitedly exclaimed over them and told me what they were. Maybe we have a little photographer budding. Eric has been saying he is going to buy her a used digital camera.

Outside the Box

Michael confirmed with me the other day that he hadn't learned to read well until grade five. He went on to say that in one of his current classes for his master's degree in counseling, they were discussing learning disabilities. Michael wasn't sure if he had a diagnosis or not when he was young. He told his online class that he thinks schools should have a more unstructured-style classroom as we did. He liked that we let him learn at his own pace.

Michael recently reminded me that I used to say to him as a young boy, "Okay, it's time to do your fifteen minutes of school."

A joke back then, and a joke now.

But not a joke when he told me recently about two high marks he got on his master's courses.

And I responded, "Good for you! I'm so glad I didn't push you when you were a young boy!"

He responded, "Yup! Now look at me—I love school!"

~ Sharon

DAY 17

Being There for Others, at Home and From Afar

Role-Modeling Through Biking

In my old folder *How to Homeschool and Make it Look Easy*, under the subject "Physical Education" and in the category of "Locomotion," I wrote, "My children love to bike."

I wrote this on April 26, 2002, and Nicole and Natasha had just turned 4 a few months earlier and were riding bikes—that is, without training wheels.

I penned at the time, "I think this is the earliest that any of the children have learned to ride."

One of the big factors was that they had watched their older siblings, which motivated them to learn. It helped too that we had a gently sloping driveway, and the girls had perfect-sized bikes.

My journaling continued with, "Now, after a week or so of practicing, they are ripping around, following Michael's rambunctious lead, and scaring me in the process. I saw Natasha wipe out, pick herself up, and move on."

My children still motivate and help each other, both in joys and sorrows.

ASSIGNMENT FOR DAY 17

Encourage your children to do some sort of service to the community, such as visiting old folks in nursing homes or being a "big sister or brother" to a younger child. Even if you can't go somewhere today, perhaps the children can write a letter to an older person from church. The list of ways to help others is limitless. Record how this went in your "Discover the Genius in Your Child" binder.

Michael (10) acted as a big brother to a youngster who was living with his grandma—Michael would play with him when they came to visit.

"...visit the fatherless and widows..." (James 1:27).

When I was a young teen, Dad encouraged me to be the principal of a girls' school—he had big dreams for me. At the time, I was skeptical of such a possibility, but his belief in what I could do helped mold the woman I have become.

Additionally, record one activity your child did on their own initiative today in your "Discover the Genius in Your Child" binder.

Clarissa's Comments | We can't visit a nursing home now during COVID-19. Eric and I have talked, though, about doing that as a family or with friends in the future and singing there. The other day, Evelyn and I stopped and talked to our elderly neighbors for a while from the end of their driveway while they stood on the porch. I love to see how Evelyn brings cheer to people with her smiles.

Families need to find some activities that they are interested in. Above all else, get a family ministry, like singing in an old folk's home or something along that line.

~ Sharon's Dad

DAY 18

Keep Your Eyes Open to Possibilities

Using Imagination to Repurpose

"Let's play office," Clarissa (8) said many years ago.

"I'll get all the good stuff in my garbage," Michael (6) said as he ran upstairs to his bedroom.

As Clarissa rooted in the office trash can, she exclaimed, "Look what I found! It's really neat!"

That's all that I recorded of their play. I imagine the two of them had a blast imitating "office" with all the supplies they unearthed.

Fast-forward to a few years ago when Eric, Clarissa's boyfriend at the time, had been living in Toronto and found some shoes on the curb for free. Next came marriage, and when Eric and Clarissa visited our place one day, somehow, these brown shoes ended up in our kitchen garbage can.

Steve came along, saw these shoes, and what do you know? He rescued them from the trash and has been wearing them ever since.

And when Eric and Clarissa moved to Toronto, they grabbed great curbside finds. The stuff looked so good that you'd never guess from where it came!

So, using imagination in childhood becomes imaginative living in adulthood.

Yes!

ASSIGNMENT FOR DAY 18

Sometime during their waking hours, in your "Discover the Genius in Your Child" binder, for ten minutes, record your children's spontaneous activities, meaning ones *they* have chosen. Keep it simple and have fun writing. Notice any themes that could indicate particular giftings that your children might have. Perhaps you will even find them creatively "repurposing" something.

"Every good gift and every perfect gift is from above, and cometh down from the Father of lights" (James 1:17a).

Clarissa's Comments | Evelyn's latest indoor hobbies are cutting, cutting, and cutting (everything and anything, such as magazines or paper), playing with playdough (she just started cutting that too!), and drawing or writing. Sometimes I find it hard to walk around her messes, but I love to see my little girl being creative. So, I step around it all and try to embrace her scattered creations.

Lighten up a tad and open your eyes to possibilities.

~ Sharon

DAY 19

New Experiences

Dreams and Ideas

Years ago, I had written: "Kayla (10) has now started violin lessons! A great dream of hers."

She had called in to the local radio station during "Swap and Shop" and asked, in her little-girl voice, if someone had a violin for sale.

She was so excited when a man phoned to speak to her, and he said that he'd give her one that he has on his wall—for free! She was thrilled. All it needed was a new bow.

We found a teacher for her and Steve. Steve had always dreamed of playing the violin as well, and then he could be her driver.

After their first lesson, the two were in the living room, practicing their homework on their violins.

I was multi-tasking in another room—standing on a stool trying to do something on a high shelf and talking on the phone. Then these first-day violinists came up to me because they wanted me to hear their first note—DDDDDDDDDD, over and over.

Needless to say, I could hardly hear the person on the other end of the phone, but I was happy to listen to the D.

At the time, my written conclusion was, "I must say, though, it is hard on the ears."

As an adult, Kayla has used her violin skills to teach violin to her sister and, more currently, to a young local student. She has also played this instrument while performing with family and/or friends in jails and at other events.

Children's youth can be a preparation for a useful and interesting life.

ASSIGNMENT FOR DAY 19

Present each child with a new project or idea. It can be a very small activity like allowing them to make *Edible Playdough* or letting them use a camera. It might be something they are interested in already or an idea they have never considered before. This helps train children to keep their options open. Record how this assignment turned out in your "Discover the Genius in Your Child" binder.

"...he should make his soul enjoy good in his labor..." (Ecc. 2:24).

My dad signed my oldest sister and me up for canoe lessons, flight training, and sewing instruction when we were teens. He even had us live with a single missionary for a few days so we could learn her bookseller's trade. I remember feeling out of place while we lived with her and tried to help her. I worried—did she really need us? What was the point in all this? I now write and sell books that I have written. Could there be a connection with my current interest in books to that time we lived with the missionary bookseller?

Looking back, I realize that this was one of Dad's efforts to present us with an array of options that we may or may not have used later in life. When our children were little, Steve and I tried to do similar things for them.

Additionally, record one activity your child did on their own initiative today in your "Discover the Genius in Your Child" binder.

Participant's Comments | I love giving my children new experiences. I guess writing them down should be the first step.

MY CONVERSATION WITH A PARTICIPANT

PARTICIPANT: I wonder what to do with children who don't want to try new things and don't have a desire to get out and do anything new. Then it turns into a "forcing" thing. Did you make your children take music lessons for a specific amount of time, like give it a try for a month? A year? Was there ever anything that your parents wanted you to do that you didn't want to do? Did you want to learn how to canoe? Or did you just do it because they told you to?

SHARON: First of all, we as parents will never get everything right. It is a kind of sink or swim situation. Trying this and trying that, finding the balance between encouraging children instead of pressuring them. I would advise moms to consider approaching new opportunities along the same lines of how my mom potty trained us—try it, see if the child is ready, and then stop if they aren't interested yet. You can always try again later. I wish I had easy answers, but I don't know if there are any. Simply present them with something and see what happens.

More About Dreams and Ideas

Nicole (11) wrote on January 1, 2010, that she wanted to "get a banjo."

We did find her a banjo, as well as an excellent teacher. By the following year, things had progressed quite a bit. She wrote in her journal that after a banjo lesson, she and Natasha practiced with two cousins for an ensemble—where Nicole played the banjo (with Natasha on violin, one cousin on piano, and another cousin singing).

Moving forward through the years, Nicole has played banjo with our family at various events.

~ Sharon

EDIBLE PLAYDOUGH

Mix:
¼ cup honey
½ cup smooth peanut butter
½ cup skim milk powder OR protein powder
2 tablespoons xylitol*

NOTE: Vary the amount of xylitol to achieve the desired consistency.

*Alternately, substitute erythritol, coconut sugar or regular icing sugar.

When children play with this, make sure their hands are clean first!

DAY 20

Order in the Chaos

Spontaneity

In the long-ago days, during my children's carefree childhood (with all its imperfections, of course!), they had plenty of spare time to be creative.

One day I heard Kayla (10) say, "We want to get ready for Kids' Club."

They bustled about.

Later I heard, "Dad, how do you sing the Zacchaeus song?" So, he wrote it out for them.

A list of duties penned in girlish handwriting detailed the following:

1. Kayla, Clarissa, Michael: in charge of the singing.
2. Kayla: in charge of the story. Michael: hold up the picture.
3. Clarissa: games, balloon games, questions.
4. Michael: coloring and water.

All was in readiness.

Then Clarissa (7) went upstairs to find Nicole (3) and Natasha (3), who were the only clients for these young missionaries. Natasha had just awoken from her nap, so Clarissa asked, "Can you say this verse?"

Natasha, still sleepy, couldn't bring herself to be meditative at the moment, so Clarissa let it pass.

"Where's Ollie (the long-ago nickname for Nicole)?" Clarissa then asked.

"Still sleeping, but you can wake her up," I said, as it was already 4:30 p.m.

Clarissa hustled the sleepy duo downstairs to the kitchen.

Clarissa slid onto the lower ledge of our kitchen step-stool, where she wrote down the students' names on the prepared attendance sheet, which was resting on the step-stool.

Next, the two 3-year-olds sat quietly side-by-side on our yellow-green kitchen chairs. They sang the Zacchaeus song. Michael played the autoharp, and the twins each played the toy drums.

Kayla then read a story about Zacchaeus, with Michael (6) holding up a picture for the girls to see. Zacchaeus' picture was colored.

I journaled at the time, "They organized themselves very well on their own."

I found out that even the Bible verse was on the Zacchaeus theme: "He received Jesus joyfully." For the balloon game, one of the "teachers" had written this verse about Zacchaeus on the balloon.

Michael said, "Hey, Mom, look! The balloons got popped." (It doesn't hurt to make learning fun, does it?)

Kayla told me, "Nicole picked from the draw, and drew her name, so she got a surprise."

As a happy conclusion, the twins nodded when I asked if they liked the Kids' Club.

Now, these young adult children of mine are still trying to find creative ways to live their current lives.

And our grandbaby, Evelyn, is already leading the next generation's pack like Kayla, as the oldest, did in our family. It will be interesting to see what organized (and chaotic) proceedings occur in my grandchildren's childhoods.

ASSIGNMENT FOR DAY 20

Sometime during their waking hours, in your "Discover the Genius in Your Child" binder, for ten minutes, record your children's spontaneous activities—ones *they* have chosen. Notice how your children play—is there order or chaos? Can you be okay with either?

Participants' Comments

PARTICIPANT 1: My two boys are tying string to Lego characters and letting them "skydive" down from the upstairs railing. My 3-year-old is constructing and playing in a small tee-pee construction in our yard and loves to make "woods stew." My 9-year-old son told me just last night, "I'm really happy with my life right now." He is the one who needs life to be slower and more spacious. He was having a tough time with his bookwork one day and asked to work in his own room. We set up a table for him, and now he does very well with focus. I was proud of him for knowing what he needed and naming it.

"And whatsoever ye do in word or deed, do all in the name of the Lord Jesus" (Col. 3:17a).

PARTICIPANT 2: After all these weeks in this course, I am seeing that 7:00 p.m. is when the children will for sure be doing something "on their own." Because of this, I will set a timer on my phone for that time to help me remember to write down their activities.

The Dance of "Freedom Versus Spontaneity"

Recently, I had written the following: "Growing up, we had lots of structure and discipline, but then, within that framework, we had lots of freedom."

I asked my family what they thought of my above statement. My one sister agreed with the freedom but not about the structure and discipline!

Then I asked mom about her version on the matter. She said, "Ladies who had more structure envied my ability to be okay with chaos."

Mom, however, asserted that she would get overwhelmed. She recently unearthed some old files that she'd been cleaning out. She dug out a few lists, with titles such as "Rules to live by" and "Rules for the family."

She said, "I think this was my attempt to make life less chaotic."

She admired her sister-in-law, who allowed freedom, but in a quiet way also had structure.

Mom said, "I didn't quite get us on a good schedule."

She concluded, "But because I'm a relaxed person with myself, maybe that stuck with you girls, rather than the lack of structure." My dear mother!

Regarding this discussion, my youngest sister said, "We all muddle along doing our best, and then once in a while, we need a reset in some areas, and that's probably what Mom's lists were about."

~ Sharon

DAY 21

Children as Entrepreneurs and Employees

Encouraging Children

Back in April 2004, I emailed my dad, "I'm glad you took me out to your shop that one time to explain how Michael (8) could do wood crafts." Before that, I remember being totally in the dark about how to help my son in this creative way.

As I remember, Dad showed me tools that Michael might need and pointed out a woodcraft that he had made as a young boy. After Dad explained some of these things to me, Steve decided to buy Michael a jigsaw. Michael put it to good use.

I kept my eyes open to see how adults decorated crafts for sale. I realized Michael could even use rough, un-sanded wood with a "country rustic, old-fashioned look." He made hearts, birds, and a bird feeder out of wood, and then I added crafty material, trying to copy what I had seen in expensive craft shops. Clarissa made dipped candles to hang from a nail on the little hearts. The final products looked so cute.

In this email to Dad, I also said, "I just wanted to say thanks because it has opened up a whole new world for Michael. He's going to try to have a craft sale at the end of the driveway sometime, with baked goods, too. Because he uses cheap or free materials, he can sell them for like one, two, or three dollars, plus people don't mind helping out a boy."

Dad responded, "Thanks for the note about Michael and his woodwork. I am glad I can be a little part of his life in this way."

Fast-forwarding to a few years ago, Dad invited Judy and me, his two oldest girls, into his office to show us where his journals are located. Just so we know.

Then he proceeded to go around the room and pointed out his artifacts, including some woodworking that he did as a boy (a very nice lamp). In his office, he also has the old cut-into chair that he used as a sawhorse. Dad said that he even sold some of his woodwork as a youth.

I asked, "Who did you sell it to?"

"Neighbors and friends, as well as to people at my parents' farmers market stand. Then I could start a bank account," Dad said. "My first attempt at entrepreneurship."

And I think of all the work involved in parenting. It reminded me a lot of my son and me many moons ago.

A while back, I bought my little great-nephew's artwork for $5. I wanted to buy it to show I was interested in his endeavors because I remembered when kind-hearted people helped Michael out. And for a worthy cause—I gave it to his great-grandparents for part of their Christmas present.

And this type of encouragement can spur on young people.

ASSIGNMENT FOR DAY 21

Teach your children not to fear hard work. Get them involved in meaningful activities, such as working for a local farmer or doing other hands-on jobs. It doesn't need to be back-breaking work, it doesn't need to be every day, and it doesn't need to pay well. Possibly your children could pull weeds or rake leaves for a neighbor. It can even be a volunteer opportunity. Record how this activity turned out in your "Discover the Genius in Your Child" binder.

"For thou shalt eat the labour of thine hands" (Ps. 128:2a).

All throughout our early teen years, my parents encouraged my sisters and me to go for a week to work on a farm two hours away. We'd come home from our hardworking experience and wonder what we could clean, cook, and bake in our own home. Mom was happy! We'd go once a summer, but it did a lot to develop my concept of work and gave us a different perspective on life.

Additionally, record one activity your child did on their own initiative today in your "Discover the Genius in Your Child" binder.

Clarissa's Comments | You and your sisters went to work for this farming family for a week. Then I told Eric that when we were young, you and Dad took us to work for them for one day. Eric thought that was funny because Evelyn and Emmett might work for these farmers for just one hour!

Michael was the boy who couldn't read in Sunday school when his buddies could. I needed to hold my head high, trusting that what we were doing was the best for him.

He was also the boy in grade five who, when we went on a sabbatical and our children went to public school that year, was "behind" most of the rest of the class. There again, I needed to stand up straight and tall. I knew exactly what we were doing by not pushing him—rushing him stressed him out.

Needless to say, he completed grade five successfully, and now, as I've said before, he's enjoying working on a master's degree in counseling for future ministry.

Is the proof in the pudding?

The key to this whole thing is to trust, trust, trust. Trust God. Trust the process. Because it felt like we were going against every grain there was to go against!

~ Sharon

DAY 22

Freedom

Homeschooling High School the Freewheelin' Way

When Kayla was going into grade six, I met with my homeschooling friend. I wanted to learn more about homeschooling high school in the same way we were doing grade school, which was going along the lines of a child's interests and not doing a lot of bookwork.

But I wondered how we would do that style of "not just workbooks" and still produce a high school diploma for our children.

My friend gave me excellent ideas, saying that the "best" or "better" type of homeschooling success stories were with families who homeschooled using a more unstructured style. These examples would be similar to our **SIFT** program—going by the child's interests and having focused studies in science, algebra, etc.

In the end, we encouraged all our children to graduate with a credited provincial secondary school diploma, as this made the most sense for us. However, we did homeschool some courses in high school using our freewheelin' style. I loved those courses. It just took a lot of record-keeping, but I didn't mind that!

Through the years, what I liked the most about our homeschooling program was the FREEDOM!

To roam the countryside around our northern home.

To travel.

To cater to individual learning styles.

To be the primary influencers of our children.

To be free.

ASSIGNMENT FOR DAY 22

Sometime during their waking hours, in your "Discover the Genius in Your Child" binder, for ten minutes, record your children's spontaneous activities—ones *they* have chosen. In order to understand your children better, rate on a scale of one to ten how interested (or uninterested!) your children appear to be in their current activity.

"Where the Spirit of the Lord is, there is liberty" (2 Cor. 3:17b).

Participants' Comments

PARTICIPANT 1: I may need to reference you in the years to come as I homeschool four boys. So far, we've been on track or ahead of track, but I doubt all four will be as easy as my first one has been.

PARTICIPANT 2: I'm glad for your reminders to be relaxed about educating our children. My daughter's science is on plants, and I've felt freer to just let her skip a bunch in the book. Yesterday we took a nature walk through the woods. She showed me where a squirrel named "Whisper" lives, she found a lovely jack-in-the-pulpit, and she checked for plants with spores or seeds all on her own. Then when we came home, she planted some flowers and chives in soil with earthworms that she had dug up.

"Dancing" Between Two Educational Systems

When Clarissa was 12, she took a break from homeschool and attended a local public school for a year. One of her teachers said, "Clarissa's transition from homeschool to public school was seamless; she fit in so well." Of course, hearing his comment made this mama proud!

~ Sharon

DAY 23

Friendships With Other Families

Socialization Is Important!

Many moons ago, I found 11-year-old Kayla's handwritten cousins-activities list of twenty things to do. This document was in preparation for when two families planned a January visit to our Kenora home.

Kayla penned these ideas: "Have a bonfire, do the twins' birthday party, play with our dress-up, play with the dog if he is still here, come to the door with our dress-up on and trick the twins, play Clue or other board or card games, skate, snowmobile, sled, make forts, play with Michael's racer car set, do plays, play computer, make stuff and sell them, make a tent out of blankets, set up tents and play in them and then sleep in them for the night, make the breakfast just the kids, ski, play outside and play inside."

By far, my favorite is Kayla's point #19: "Michael and [boy cousin] do somersaults onto the pillows, and we cheer."

It makes me wonder how (if they got around to point #19!) this cheering from the sisters and girl cousins might have boosted these young boys' egos! Maybe even this girlish adoration helped them become the fine gentlemen they are today.

ASSIGNMENT FOR DAY 23

Arrange to play a sport or activity with one or more families. This focus keeps perspective on competition. For most of us, playing professional sports is an impossible dream, but what about sports as a way of reaching out to less fortunate youngsters? Record how this activity turned out in your "Discover the Genius in Your Child" binder.

"God setteth the solitary in families" (Ps. 68:6a).

When our children were young, we heard about some local boys who thought outside the box and started a boys' club. Part of the time, they would play road hockey. Similarly, we encouraged our children to find ways to put their agile, sporty, physical make-up to good use. Some of them went with Steve to a local facility for troubled juveniles when they were in their teens. While there, they played basketball or some other sport with the youth.

Additionally, record one activity your child did on their own initiative today in your "Discover the Genius in Your Child" binder.

Even if you are unsure about the concepts in this course, try experimenting with them for this month—what will it hurt? If you don't like the results, you can go back to how you were doing things before!

~ Sharon

DAY 24

On Dabbling

Try This, Try That

Dabbling is my style. Sometimes I'm studying how to make money, and sometimes money's the last thing on my mind. (It's a good thing that Steve doesn't "dabble" in money, as he runs our finances!) Sometimes I'm into reading about how to eat healthfully—other times, I'm excited about learning how to cure my nearsightedness.

Encouraging "dabbling" is part of my homeschooling/parenting philosophy. Life's too short to stick to something just because you started it. Try this, drop that, pick up this hobby. If it gets boring, move on to another idea.

Many Januarys ago, during our homeschooling years, I wrote a little blurb that details further my dabbling theory.

Here is the story:

> *Kayla (10) had her first practice with a group of students where she was learning the French horn. After she got home, Steve and I were upstairs, listening to her bellowing away in our home office, and we were dying laugh-*

ing. The resulting sound was a combination of a foghorn and a bullfrog.

The staff thought she was doing well and had the talent for it. These instrumental lessons were held at the high school in town but for grades 5–9. In one hour, during her first class, she ranged from wanting to play the French horn, next the clarinet, then the flute, and eventually back to her original favorite, the French horn.

One helper said, "Let her decide, and if she doesn't want to stick to an instrument, let her change. It doesn't pay for her to play one she doesn't like." Fits my dabbling theory, doesn't it?

At home, when Michael (6) heard Kayla practicing, he said, "Mommy, I am getting sick of hearing that noise." (Poor boy!)

Kayla eventually gave up playing the noisy thing and moved on to other hobbies. But could it have been one of the many life experiences that helped her find her current dream job?

ASSIGNMENT FOR DAY 24

Present each child with a "device" (aka a useful toy) of some sort. Ideas could be a camera, tape recorder, computer program, or musical instrument. See if something "clicks" with a particular child. Record the results in your "Discover the Genius in Your Child" binder.

For example, through the years, I have realized that Clarissa, my second born, is "techy"—she loves cameras, cellphones, and computers.

"I will guide thee with mine eye" (Ps. 32:8b).

Additionally, record one activity your child did on their own initiative today in your "Discover the Genius in Your Child" binder.

MY CONVERSATION WITH A PARTICIPANT

PARTICIPANT: What about the child who tries every other thing but doesn't stick at anything long enough to learn to do anything well? A musical instrument, for example—would you make them stick it out for a certain length of time even if they decide it's not what they want after the third lesson? Like the child who gives up whenever something gets hard or slightly monotonous?

SHARON: I hear you! I would point you back to Day 6 and Day 19 of this course for you to re-read some of my comments to past participants. A few of my thoughts there could similarly answer your question here.

Exploring Musical Interests

Once upon a time, I taught Michael to play guitar. Then Steve and I made it possible for him to play guitar in two festivals as a young guy. Now my son has surpassed me with using bar chords and by playing an electric guitar. Recently, I was moved to tears to think of how we, as parents, encouraging him to follow the lines of his interest in guitar has led to this becoming a ministry for him.

Michael also writes songs. A few years ago, his best friend and cousin died, and Michael wrote multiple songs to help himself process his grief, using his guitar skills to accompany his singing.

~ Sharon

DAY 25

Intentionally Working on Inner Growth and Relationships

Getting Help

One day many moons ago, 9-year-old Clarissa got sick of having Nicole (5) and Natasha (5) fight over whose turn it was to do things with her, so she made up a chart. On Sunday, it was Natasha's day to spend time with Clarissa, then Monday, Nicole's turn, and so on for the rest of the week. Well, that's one way of solving problems! I didn't record in my old file if this plan was successful or not. But my daughters are all some of each other's best friends today, so maybe at least the effort helped.

I'll take this chance to put in a plug for "getting counseling," or getting help, somehow or other, if you need it—and don't we all?

Sadly, adults can "fight"—though perhaps in a more sophisticated way than children.

Or sometimes folks just get plain old stuck. (At least I do!)

I would vote for getting this help when your children are young, better yet, even before they are born! We all will fail, but the point is to minimize the damage—that's the key.

Steve and I have gotten help in various shapes and forms over the years, and I have seen a change in Steve. (And I hope in myself!)

I have observed huge positive shifts in my parents, too, as they keep working on their issues. It's never too late!

The point is not necessarily who you go to or to use a particular program or if you put down money or not. It's more the idea of laying your issues all out on the table and asking, "Here we are, and where do we want to go from here?"

No holding back!

It's a great feeling!

And it's not about arriving somewhere and being done. Nope! It's about continuing to grow with God's help.

There's my sales pitch. (Though I have no sale!)

ASSIGNMENT FOR DAY 25

Plan a visit with a smart friend, a pastor, or a professional counselor. This assignment could be you, or you and your spouse, or you as a family. My growing-up family did all of these.

You probably won't be able to do the above on the day you are reading this. The point is to start planning it. I can't see how it could hurt! Record any thoughts about today's assignment in your "Discover the Genius in Your Child" binder.

"Confess your faults one to another, and pray one for another, that ye may be healed" (James 5:16a).

Steve and I have each chosen to talk with a wise friend about personal problems, marriage issues, and/or child-rearing ideas. When I was growing up, my sisters and I were encouraged to find someone to counsel with concerning any emotional struggles we may have had. This goes a long way in overcoming obstacles to fulfilling our God-given potential. It is amazing how emotional problems can hinder a person's energy level and creative output.

Additionally, record one activity your child did on their own initiative today in your "Discover the Genius in Your Child" binder.

When our children were young, we tried for Steve and me to take them individually on "dates." Even though we had five children and were busy parents, we knew that alone time with dad or mom was worth carving out time for.

As an example, in Natasha's "life notebook" (we started the project of keeping track of important events in these books for our children when they were young), Steve wrote that he and Natasha (6) on a March day in 2004 "went on date. We ate chips and pop [from the chip wagon]." They also drove "to the ice road and saw a big hole as you go on the ice." Steve then penned that Natasha was "very talkative and could hardly wait till we went on our date." She even "sat in the car, waiting for me."

~ Sharon

Clarissa's Comments | Eric and I have wanted to start going on father/child and mother/child dates with our children. This is a good reminder for me to start doing it with Evelyn soon. Reading this also inspired me to think of getting a mentor.

Participant's Comments | Each month one parent goes out with one child. I appreciated your advice to not be afraid of getting counseling input as a couple, too.

DAY 26

Best Learning Comes by Allowing Children to Freely Go by Their Interests

When Kayla, our oldest, was in high school, and we were homeschooling her in grade ten, I wrote up a five-point list that detailed our philosophy and program we were going by. I will, in this and the next four days, be detailing these points one by one.

*Concluding Point #1 of Our **SIFT** Educational Philosophy*

We believe that children learn best when they can freely pursue their passions, interests, and gifts with their own learning style.

- When such child-focused learning can be integrated with our province's ministry of education guidelines, we feel this provides children with a well-rounded curriculum. This process successfully prepares children to meet life as adults.

- We believe that eclectic education provides a superior education, where the best in various teaching methods are employed for the individual child.

Kayla is always attentive in class and willing to help her classmates with a smile. Kayla, you're an asset to our class—keep up the great work!

~ Kayla's long-ago high school public school teacher (on a special note sent home concerning having received one of the highest marks in the class on her final exam)

DOCUMENTING FUN PHYS-ED

In our (seemingly) carefree homeschooling program, I would record how various activities fit under different "subjects." This process made me feel better about creating a stimulating homeschooling environment without being overly structured. I loved writing as well, so this was a fun pastime for me.

Inside my old folder, *How to Homeschool and Make It Look Easy*, I had filed a category labeled "Phys-Ed." As our children explored our large yard and surrounding bush, I knew that they were getting lots of physical exercise.

In our province's curriculum guidelines for physical education, children were to demonstrate movement skills. So, one April day in 2002, I recorded 7-year-old Michael's biking escapade. I was sitting on a lawn chair with my feet propped up on another lawn chair. A third lawn chair sat a few yards away. Michael, on his bike, would whiz in this space between this third lawn chair and me.

He was definitely practicing his movement ability!

I wondered at the time if Michael rode this obstacle course to impress his mother. I penned that I was actually worried for my safety.

But I survived, and he thrived. And here he is, currently whizzing a zero-turn lawn tractor for his lawn care business.

ASSIGNMENT FOR DAY 26

Sometime during their waking hours, in your "Discover the Genius in Your Child" binder, for ten minutes, record your children's spontaneous activities—ones *they* have chosen. Notice if they stick to one activity, even for days, or if they frequently vary what they are doing.

Clarissa's Comments | As a child, I remember doing the same thing day after day, like fixing our raft and frog catching. After a while, we would move on to playing little people and building farms out on the grass. Then it would be building huge snow forts and playing motel in the snow for days on end. Or it

"And all thy children shall be taught of the Lord; and great shall be the peace of thy children" (Is. 54:13).

would be clubs and plays and everything else in between. My memory is that we would get very into one activity and spend most of our time doing that, until weeks later we would move onto the next.

I want our children to have the carefree childhood to explore and play that I had.

I told Mom the other day, "I still like to 'play.'" I get my work done quickly, so I can do what I love, which includes experimenting with sourdough baking, being outside with my children, writing, doing watercolor, or playing piano when I am in the mood. I think of most of my work as my "play," even now as an adult. It makes life fun, and I believe it was because of my carefree childhood, where I had lots of room to explore, that I can do that today.

One day as I sat outside to get some fresh air, I was thinking about the childhood I had, and the way my parents schooled us. It has hugely shaped who I am today and how I view life.

DAY 27

Learning Through Life

*Concluding Point #2 of Our **SIFT** Educational Philosophy*

We believe education transpires best when children can learn through life. Because of this, our school provides structured classes integrated with life-learning experiences.

- This means "school" can happen 24/7.
- During our homeschooling years, we traveled extensively while living in northern Ontario. Homeschooling nicely fit our educational style as many learning experiences occurred while experiencing the country first-hand.
- Part of this homeschooling philosophy means that we believe that children (and adults!) learn to read by reading, to sing by singing, to write by writing, and the list goes on.

LEARNING MUSIC BY MAKING MUSIC

Recently someone asked me, "So, how did you do homeschooling? What did it look like?"

For one thing, I would do lots of journaling to keep track of our children's learning in life. Below is an example of how I recorded life-learning in the following long-ago story, which I entitled, "Have Your Fling."

"Mom, come to the concert," Clarissa (9) had said.

So, on this January day in 2003, I dropped what I was doing—it was my motherly duty. Plus, I thoroughly enjoyed watching my children's hilariously creative projects.

I headed over to the bottom of the steps where the audience could watch.

Our indoor stairway has steps going up to a landing, then you do a ninety-degree turn and go up more stairs to our second floor.

I watched Nicole (5), where she stood on the middle landing, singing two solos. Next, Natasha (5) sang one song, then Nicole one more.

I penned at the time, "Not sure about the overbalance of Nicole, but I suppose life is not always fair, as long as the balance is not always tipped one way."

Michael (7) and Clarissa were busy at the top of the steps, somewhere out of view, doing the backstage percussion. They were using light blue, dark blue, and red ribbons, left-over from our wedding thirteen years previously. The children had also tied a kitchen knife to one string and a cymbal to another, operated by Michael. Problems occurred as first, a knife fell, then his cymbal.

Clarissa operated a little old tin teapot, banged with a cymbal, and both items tied together on one string.

As they sang on the middle landing, each twin operated a sort of pulley system with a bell way up on the top level.

It was quite funny. I shielded my head part of the time for fear of a knife flinging at me. I developed a side ache from laughter.

At some point, Kayla (11) had joined me and was watching, too.

"Darling, you've got to come!" I eventually called to Steve.

He came over, shielding his ears.

Finally, Clarissa announced, "We're done!" as she bounced down the stairs.

Afterward, there were remnants of string, hanging

down toward the bottom of the steps where I stood, with a cymbal tied on the end along with two knives.

At the time, I wrote that these misplaced items "stand monument (until it all gets cleaned up) to some morning fun when my children had their fling with knives flying and cymbals banging. It's one more memory for them and me of a free childhood with hardly a care in the world."

Hence, children (and adults) learn through life as they follow their dreams and pursue their God-given interests.

ASSIGNMENT FOR DAY 27

As a parent, integrate an activity that you are really interested in doing into your day, even if it's only for ten minutes. Children can learn from seeing parents being creative in pursuing their passions. Record how this went in your "Discover the Genius in Your Child" binder.

"[God] giveth us richly all things to enjoy" (1 Tim. 6:17b).

For example, I began writing books when my children were young. Back in the day, my writing perhaps inspired Clarissa because she also began writing a book. While a mother pursuing her own interests can be overdone, especially with my get-up-and-go personality and drive, it can also inspire your children. To keep this in balance during our homeschooling years, I would talk to Steve occasionally to see if he thought I was at the computer too much.

When I was wallpapering our little house years ago, I was telling Mom about my undertaking. She said, "That's good for your children to see you enjoying a project like that." Hobbies or doing things we love help bring a passion to our lives, and our children will hopefully model this behavior.

Additionally, record one activity your child did on their own initiative today in your "Discover the Genius in Your Child" binder.

Participant's Comments | I like this assignment. I did actually get to do something today that I enjoy—making simple cards. I did it with my 7-year-old as an activity for just him and me during quiet time and to see if it's something he could make to sell. He's made a lot of cards on his own for people, but I wanted to guide him a tad more if he is going to sell them. He kept saying how fun it was and then later worked on some alone.

When Clarissa was 12 and attended public school for a year, her teacher told me, "Whatever you did in your homeschool worked. I wish I could send some of my students to go through your program first before they come to me." Yay! "Go me," as my girls would say.

~ Sharon

DAY 28

Training Children for the Future

Concluding Point #3 of Our ***SIFT*** *Educational Philosophy*

We believe that parents pass on their faith and practice best when they teach their own children values, morals, and proper behavior. Hence, we incorporate these life concepts into their "education" in order for them to enter life as independent and responsible citizens. As usual with our program's focus, it's important all along to go by the child's readiness and interest.

> This summer, I was impressed with the poise of your two teenage daughters.
>
> *An uncle (referring to my two oldest daughters, many moons ago)*

Your big girls are so smart. I think it's because they're homeschooled.

Their grandfather, Clair (long ago, referring to Kayla and Clarissa)

LIFE LESSONS FROM A LEMONADE STAND

Kayla (9) and Clarissa (6) had been talking about having a lemonade stand. When I saw a can of low-cost lemonade mix at the store and said, "You can get some for your stand," they were more thrilled than if I had offered them candy.

After arriving home, I heard "Lemonade" and "Let's make a sign" and "May we use our little picnic table like we've seen other children do?" I didn't think too much more about it, as I scurried around doing my duties until I was casually informed that they were in business. They were? I hurried outside to watch this demonstration of independence. Sure enough, a sign in scrawly print, "Lemonade Stand, 10 Cents a glass," directed customers to the sale. People driving by were actually stopping and doing business with *my* children. When a prospective customer approached, the girls quickly sat up, and Michael (5) ran back from his play to plop into position. In between sales, I quickly re-combed my 2-year-old girls' stribbly hair (my twin daughters had joined the fun) while telling Michael, "Go and wash your hands." Then I retreated into the background once again.

A neighbor came by the second time because it was "so good." Another car stopped and another. One mother dropped in and got lemonade for her children on their way home from school. This activity was all going on without much help from me!

They sat in the bright sun for two hours until the inspiration faded as the customers and cold lemonade supply dwindled. Kayla then hauled in the food supplies while calling behind her, "Clarissa, bring in the table."

My children had done most of this project (from start to finish) on their own. It reminded me of the day that I knew would be coming all too soon when they would be gone. My little ones were becoming more independent daily, including operating their own citrus drink business.

Sometimes I would get discouraged—was my motherly training doing any good? But when I saw how well they were starting to work without me, it gave me the courage to keep training with, "Don't splash water on the twins!" and "Be nice to the cat!"

I would, for a while yet, need to answer questions like, "You mean God always was?!" and "Is a bad man going to come into our house tonight?" They were still so little—I enjoyed giving them a mother's guidance and love.

But as my children continued to have unaided lemonade sales, serving customers with graciousness, saying, "You can have the second glass for free," I saw into the future the way God wanted me to see. This venture was life training—not just for that day. I knew they were there today but gone tomorrow.

I prayed back then that my children would continue to seek God like the time when Michael, after I told him to pray that he would find a particular toy at a garage sale, responded, "I did already." Or like the day when Clarissa said sweetly, "I prayed to God to help me find my dolly, and here I looked, and there she was!"

In those long-ago days, I felt that if the world could see in my children the breath of God and would know the miracle of lives lived with Heaven in view, my effort would be rewarded. And it paid off—my five children who were trailing after me and having successful lemonade stands did become less dependent on me, learning all the while to become fully dependent on the hand of God.

The marvelous fact is that these concepts are being passed down the generations. Last summer Evelyn (2) had her own little lemonade stand at the end of their laneway. Her parents are "schooling" her and her brother through life, too—with the greatest focus being on raising them to love God and grow up to serve Him.

ASSIGNMENT FOR DAY 28

Once again, record any interests you see your children enjoying today in your "Discover the Genius in Your Child" binder. But beware, they may change daily. The point is not to pigeonhole your children into a particular activity just because you noticed that interest at one time in their lives. Remember that you are training for the future, and there's plenty of time for them to decide on their life work and calling.

"Bring [your children] up in the nurture and admonition of the Lord" (Eph. 6:4b).

As an example, in May 2004, I had written that I noticed the following interests/life skills in my three oldest children:

Kayla (13)

-teaching

-tidying up

Clarissa (10)

-art (she draws a lot)

-love of nurturing children (e.g., babysitting)

-entertaining Nicole and Natasha

Michael (9)

-art (he likes to draw)

-sports

Participant's Comments | I have always loved watching what my children enjoy. This month I have been more observant, and it confirmed a lot of the things I've been seeing. For our 5-year-old, his favorite things have stayed the same for a couple of years now. I am excited to see how they will play out in his adult life. Our youngest is 3, and I feel he has some things he plays with all the time, but there is a new bigger world opening for him. He spends hours pedaling his little bike up and down the driveway and around the patio. He is so proud he can bike. I'm excited to see how the next couple of years shape him.

DAY 29

Children Learn by Teaching Others

Concluding Point #4 of Our ***SIFT*** *Educational Philosophy*

We believe that when a person teaches a subject, the child/youth/adult learns as much as or more than if they were simply taught the knowledge. Because of this, when one of our students teaches younger students, we consider that "school."

> *To teach something, you need to understand the subject material. It also reinforces the concepts you have learned in the past.*
>
> *~ former homeschool mom, who also happens to be my sister*

OLDER TEACHING YOUNGER BASIC LIFE SKILLS: FIRE-BUILDING, FOOD, AND FUN

I have a blue folder from December 2003 (during our homeschooling years) with a piece of lined paper with 12-year-old Kayla's red handwriting.

The title says: "Campfire Club" (which probably was including her four younger siblings).

It lists the snacks: hot chocolate and hot dogs (quite obviously needing a hot campfire for those).

"It's just a club. It will be a fun club." (Glad to get that straight!)

Following that, Kayla penned, "You may not forget your badge. (The badges were cut-out colored circles with the person's name, as well as "c.f.c.".) The password for this week is 'adventure.' We will just talk about fun stuff to do."

Then her final words: "Have a great time."

So, how did this escapade conclude?

She told me afterward that they made a fire, but they didn't get it going really well—she wanted to do this, but it was too hard.

(I wonder, then, if the disappointed crew just ate the snacks cold?)

So, what if it didn't fly? She at least got a start and had fun in the process.

ASSIGNMENT FOR DAY 29

Decide on and write down in your "Discover the Genius in Your Child" binder one activity each child needs or wants to pursue OR a piece of equipment you need to beg, buy, or borrow in order for them to delve into an area of their dreams. Slate a time in the near future when you will obtain whatever materials each child needs.

"Thou art my trust from my youth" (Ps. 71:5b).

Then, if possible, try having an older child involve one of the younger siblings in their chosen activity. Once your child gets this accomplished, record what you have learned about each of them during this process.

Additionally, record one activity your child did on their own initiative today in your "Discover the Genius in Your Child" binder.

Folks, you are almost at the end of the book!
Here are my ideas as you move forward:

Have patience
Go by your gut
Trust God
Go by the interest and inclination and desire of each child
Get smart people on board with you and your plan
Have fun in the process and enjoy the ride
Take one step at a time

Hopefully, my **SIFT** *program has been helpful in learning some of the practical tips of how our family got from A to Z. We always had a goal in front of our faces and eventually got there! Your goal might be different than ours, but that doesn't really matter. The point is to have a destination, so you know where to head, and then eventually, to know when you have arrived!*

~ Sharon

DAY 30

Last Lesson and Farewell

Concluding Point #5 of Our ***SIFT*** *Educational Philosophy*

We believe that **socialization is essential** for the development of a well-balanced child; therefore, plenty of interaction with others outside the immediate family is imperative. A family should not be stuck in a house between four walls, but rather be willing to think outside the box about encouraging children to be active with a broad range of social groups. For this reason, we involved our children in various formal and informal settings for interaction with others.

> **Participant's Comments** | Interesting that this is the concluding point, as just today we invited a 7-year-old church friend over for three hours this afternoon (before I read this!). It motivated us all to get chores done this morning. I find that once the friend is here, I learn so much more about my children—what they need to learn about treating friends first and doing things they might not enjoy as much.

GETTING OUT OF FOUR WALLS AND BROADENING THE VIEW

I don't like to plop all my eggs in one basket, but rather pick eggs from a variety of baskets in order to keep a broad worldview.

My parents taught me this while I was young. They didn't "sink their teeth" into only one famous preacher/counselor/seminar teacher's teaching nor jump our family onto just one bandwagon, whether it was on time management or about how we should then live or on life principles.

Instead, Dad and Mom took us to a famous counselor's seminar, a speech by a time management consultant, and a life principle's seminar. As a young teen, I rebelled against going to the latter one, and my dad let me sit out rather than in. I was fuming about being boxed in and controlled by lists, but thankfully, my dad was open-minded, let me fuss, and didn't force me to sit in the seminar. Was it because Dad freed me up that later I ended up attending the seminar and, through the years, was blessed?

Mom also supported Dad in not going to extremes, and this "not laying all our eggs in one basket" (and rather dabbling in various opportunities) helped me see that God can move and work in multiple ways.

So, rather than not going to a particular seminar because I don't agree with everything the speaker says, I will go and get whatever blessing I can. I won't agree with everyone about everything. Hopefully, the variety of opportunities will keep my heart and mind open to a load of truths.

This method seems to keep me balanced and from going crazy one way or the other, except going crazy for God—can't go wrong there!

Participant's Comment | This quote about not having all my eggs in one basket is good for me because I'm not so much that way—I'm more structured.

ASSIGNMENT FOR DAY 30

Congratulate yourself! You made it! You've reached the goal of getting through this program.

Go somewhere by yourself and evaluate how this is going to change you and the lives of your children. I like to go out for tea to "get away from it all."

In your day planner, mark a date in six months to a year from now to go through this program again. Mold it to fit your needs. When it's time to go through it the second time, write your own book like I am doing ☺.

"The Lord bless thee, and keep thee" (Num. 6:24).

One last time, record an activity your child did on their own initiative today. Record this final day's journaling from Day 30 in your "Discover the Genius in Your Child" binder.

We're blessed to meet so many people, but that's part of me wanting to learn and keep good friends. This was passed on to you as well, praise the Lord, because all that helps to increase one's knowledge, horizons, and visions. Learn, have good challenging friends, love the Lord, and one's life will bless many.

~ Sharon's Dad

Conclusion

Several years ago, when I was sitting in a local coffee shop, a man who was leaving the restaurant said, "You have your work cut out for you."

My feet were up on a chair, and on the table in front of me was a teacup, along with my day planner, a stack of folders, my computer, and my phone. Did I look like a woman on a mission? I was!

I had been posting about our various **SIFT** parenting/homeschooling ideas and philosophies for my Facebook readers. My dream with writing that flurry of homeschooling chronicles was so that, at the very least, I could put the stories into a book for our family. I also desired to get the word out for young moms.

Clarissa told me it would be fun if I'd put out my third homeschooling book after our family was done homeschooling. At the time, I was happy I was at least getting some of these oldie goldie stories into more of an orderly format rather than simply stuck in my ancient folders.

Fast-forward a few years—most of those stories have found their way into the book you have just read. With these tales fleshing out our **SIFT** method, I'm not implying that people have to do homeschooling or parenting precisely as we did. That isn't the point! We all need to be ourselves. But I would love to offer permission (if anyone needs it!) to color outside the lines. One friend said that when she thinks of me, she pictures a coloring page with bright colors but not colored in the lines. Another friend called me quirky!

Ok! Obviously, you wouldn't want everyone to be like me—the point is to be yourself. To let yourself go!

And whatever you do, when you try out the ideas I've presented here, remember:

- Have fun!
- Try this, try that. Experiment, experiment, experiment.
- Don't let someone else, including this program, put you in a box. You are the expert on your children/family.
- Trust the process, trust God, trust yourself, trust your children—and let 'er rip!

Farewell, you dear readers who have joined me. I wish you the best with your families and your children's education! Feel free to re-do this program whenever you want inspiration!

God bless!

-Sharon Schnupp Kuepfer

By the end of these thirty days, if:

You are a little freer
Your child is a little freer
You have allowed your child to try more things
You feel more headspace to dream big, even for yourself, because these concepts work for us as adults, too
Your children are dreaming bigger
You are letting go of perfectionism
You see your child learning through life
Your children are happier and more relaxed and more who God intended them to be
You feel more flexibility in your life
You have created a bit more of a stimulating environment
Your children are learning naturally when they are ready
You and your children are "finding yourselves"
You and your children are pursuing your passions
Any or all of the above has been incorporated into your life

Then I will be happy because I will have accomplished what I set out to do ☺.

~ Sharon

APPENDIX I

On Using "Educational Lingo"

I loved recording things, using "educational lingo," so I could "prove," even if only to myself, that my children were learning. Here's one such (very detailed!) report I wrote about Kayla (10).

- *The capitalized subject categories generally followed our provincial educational guidelines.*
- *It is not a report card, which details her problem areas. Instead, it was a fun way that I, as a teacher teacher–mother, documented her learning.*

KAYLA'S SCHOOL REPORT

Kayla (10) has the ability to move in and out with ease through the various compartments of life (another name for school subjects), successfully making the lines of distinction barely visible. To me, this is one of the qualities required for living life to its full potential.

For MUSIC, she has experimented with the recorder, has become efficient at playing the autoharp, and has specialized in the piano (both in classical music and as an accompanist for hymns). Besides this, she sings regularly, with good range, tone, and pitch. She also has taken beginner theory.

For ART, she enjoys using a variety of materials and mediums to express herself. She chooses appropriate and vivid colors to make a nice picture or map. She can follow directions to make little decorative boxes out of paper with matching lids. She had art instruction with a Kenora watercolor artist and has produced watercolors that decorate our house. She loves to go through the house and tidy, finishing off her efforts artistically by lighting candles.

Kayla has a love for PRESENTATIONS. She coordinates various acts, musicals, and plays with her siblings or friends. She is, with great enthusiasm and effort, getting prepared with her siblings for a Christmas play, including props, script, actors, and costumes. She is also participating in a church Christmas program.

Kayla has learned HEALTHY LIVING skills when she took a babysitter course that included a beginner version of CPR. She takes care when she operates the stove, oven, and microwave. The doctor gave her a fit bill of health when he said she has a strong, healthy body. "She must not eat a lot of hamburgers and fries," he said. She has an appropriate concern about getting various hereditary illnesses (hypoglycemia, diabetes) and tries to eat good foods without a lot of sugar. She knows how to convert a regular recipe to a more healthful version using raw sugar, carob chips, and 60% whole wheat flour. She participated in a Meal Etiquette Course, with the finale being a trip to a fancy, ninth-floor restaurant overlooking Lake of the Woods in Kenora.

Kayla regularly participates in PHYSICAL EDUCATION—swimming lessons, biking, group ball games, hikes, boating, sledding, skating, fishing, golfing, and other outdoor pursuits.

ACTIVE PARTICIPATION is a natural part of Kayla's existence. She loves being involved socially with siblings, friends, and cousins. She performs at homeschool presentations, at performances our family gives at a seniors' "club day away," and at church functions. She often participates in learning activities with others.

WRITING comes naturally for Kayla as she writes on a daily basis—letters to friends, emails, lists of projects, or daily details. Writing for her school assignments is well done and adds credibility to her portfolio. She completed a spelling diagnostic test at the beginning of this year which placed her at or above her age level. She writes neatly in both manuscript and cursive and has taken typing training on a computer course as well. She has completed the Canadian Achievement Test since we started homeschooling that shows her successful standing in her appropriate grade level in the basic subjects.

She loves to READ and breezes through a variety of reading materials for pleasure and information both silently and orally. Her range is broad and useful for whatever need arises—recipes, *Reader's Digest* articles, storybooks, and letters or emails from friends. The other day she told me, "Mom, I read three books so far today." She also does reading for "school" research.

For ORAL AND VISUAL COMMUNICATION, Kayla has experience with the tape recorder, the phone, the camera, and the computer. She is working on a cut and paste memories photo album. She successfully organizes and plans Kids' Club for her twin sisters and other children who visit. She has a lot of practice with oral communication when she teaches and entertains her twin sisters, giving them instructions. She also coordinates various elaborate scenarios she and her siblings are involved in bringing to life, such as "Hotel," "Store," and "Bank."

Various mathematical concepts (such as numeration, geometry, and measurement) are covered in her MATH textbook or on a more realistic basis in life—baking, telling time, computer work, earning money (and counting it, as well as keeping track of her earnings in her own bank book), puzzles, games, and manipulatives.

For SCIENCE, Kayla has covered the study of heat and motion in a structured course. She has experimented with kitchen chemistry and studies backyard biology (e.g., building an ant observation center). She has participated in various field trips, including The Great Canadian Mining Show and a partially guided hike in the Vernon Nature Trails in Kenora.

Kayla has explored various phases of SOCIAL STUDIES, including heritage and citizenship and Canada and world connections. Early civilizations is covered in our regular family Bible Study. For practical experience, she took a field trip to Banff with her grandparents and toured

Lower Fort Garry, Mennonite Village Museum, Kenora Museum, Children's Museum in Winnipeg, and the Mather Walls Historical House in Kenora.

I have confidence that Kayla could enter the world of work or study (a job or college) even with no further book knowledge as long as she continues with life learning at her current pace. Given the fact she is only 10, she still has lots of time to freely explore her environment while continuing to acquire knowledge. Although we do the school stuff, what's really important seems to be coming from life and following her interests.*

Clarissa's Comments | I love this. I think that this could be written about any child. Growing up, we were given lots of room to explore, and almost everything could be counted as learning and school.

Participant's Comments | All that by 10? Seems impressive.

*My thought is that anyone could write up a similar report on their child since everyone has a God-given, creative nature and desire for learning.

APPENDIX II

A Bit More on Homeschooling High School

In a video chat during my April 2020 course, *30 Days to Discover the Genius in Your Child*, one participant said it would be nice to know how we did schooling as the children got older. Here's a bit of a summary.

We kind of muddled along bit by bit, year by year, research after research, talking with other homeschooling parents and staff in local high schools. Just like the rest of parenting, we meandered along with the goal in mind of "getting our children through high school." And we got there!

For high school, Kayla and Clarissa did a combination of homeschooled courses, which were accepted by the local high school, along with alternate and mainstream classroom education courses within the public system. Michael chose to do all his high school in the alternate educational program through the local high school.

In grades nine and ten, Nicole and Natasha did math and English (I always felt these two subjects were essential to "get right") with an alternate education program from the local high school, along with two more of the school's courses. The remaining courses we homeschooled, going along the lines of their interests. Subjects like "Phys-Ed" and "Food and Nutrition" were fun ones to count hours for activities that fit into these subject categories. Then when the girls got to grade eleven, the local high school principal wanted them to do all their courses with the local high school in order to graduate with their diploma, which the girls did.

All five of our children graduated with a recognized high school diploma, which Steve and I had wanted for them—and our children wanted, too. They have all gone on to higher education and easily gotten into their chosen post-secondary schools with their recognized diplomas.

I had explained much of the above in detail to my friend so she could have ideas for how to help her 16-year-old—coming from a homeschooled and private school background—get into college. At the end of our conversation, she said she realized that our story was good for her to hear because no way was perfect or without struggle. Just like any family, we simply did the best we could.

Afterward, she emailed, "Thanks again for the chat. I feel like I got good direction and hats off to you for pulling/pushing/helping your children through the maze!"

And I agree, yes, it was a maze. But well worth the work to be on the other side of all that now. We reached our goal, and wow, what a great feeling!

Acknowledgments

My darling (Steve) has been there with me throughout this journey, during both the cloudy and the sunny days. While I did most of the "schoolish" aspect of our children's schooling, I have always leaned on his support. After I read through most of an early draft of this book to him, he said, "It is an awesome curriculum—following a child's interests. It's what formed our children. We didn't push them. They did well with it and loved it. And they all went on, and some are still going, to university or college and have gotten along fine. Our children are thriving in what they want to do."

Index

RECIPES

ASSIGNMENTS

ALSO BY
Sharon Schnupp Kuepfer

SHARON'S LEGACY SERIES

Homeschooling Years
(The Kuepfer Family)

Homeschooling Moments and Child-Friendly Recipes:
A Collection of the Unique Adventures of a Mennonite Family

There's No Place Like Home:
Tales and Treats from a Mennonite Family

Little Prairie Girl Series
(Sharon's mother's childhood)

Little Prairie Girl: Are We Rich or Poor?

Little Prairie Girl Growing Up: Moving!

Little Pennsylvania Dutch Boy Series
(Sharon's father's childhood)

Little Pennsylvania Dutch Boy: Will the War Ever End?

Little Pennsylvania Dutch Boy Growing Up: Will the Vision Die?

Pennsylvania Girl Series
(Sharon's paternal grandmother's childhood)

Lena of Terre Hill

Mennonite Girl from Russia Series
(Sharon's maternal grandmother's childhood)

Sarah in the Village

Northern Girl Series
(Sharon's childhood)

At the Brown House on the Corner

30 Days to Discover the Genius in Your Child: Equipping Your Children for Life

---

You may contact Sharon Schnupp Kuepfer via her website

www.skuepfer.com

or on Facebook.

Made in the USA
Middletown, DE
19 December 2021

56568012R00093